The Mediterranean Diet Cookbook for Beginners

1800 Delicious and Healthy Mediterranean Recipes for a Balanced Lifestyle, 28 Days Meal Plan to Lose Weight and Build Healthy Habits

Tabatha Coughlin

Copyright © 2023 by Tabatha Coughlin All rights reserved.

All Rights Reserved.

The content contained within this book may not be reproduced, duplicated, or transmitted without direct written permission from the author or the publisher. Under no circumstances will any blame or legal responsibility be held against the publisher, or author, for any damages, reparation, or monetary loss due to the information contained within this book, either directly or indirectly.

Legal Notice: This book is copyright protected. It is only for personal use. You cannot amend, distribute, sell, use, quote or paraphrase any part, or the content within this book, without the consent of the author or publisher

CONTENTS

Introduction 6
What exactly is the Mediterranean Diet? 6
What are the benefits of the Mediterranean Diet? 6
How to get started with a Mediterranean Diet? 6

Measurement Conversions 7

Breakfast Recipes Recipes 9
Feta & Olive Breakfast 10
Classic Shakshuka 10
Yummy Lentil Stuffed Pitas 10
Veg Mix And Blackeye Pea Burritos 11
Baked Eggs In Avocado 11
Red Pepper Coques With Pine Nuts 12
Morning Pizza Frittata 12
Mushroom And Caramelized Onion Musakhan 13
Tomato Eggs With Fried Potatoes 13
Hot Zucchini & Egg Nests 14
Citrus French Toasts 14
Basil Cheese Omelet 14
Lemon Cardamom Buckwheat Pancakes 15
Strawberry Basil Mascarpone Toast 15
Berry-yogurt Smoothie 15
Chocolate-strawberry Smoothie 15
Cheesy Broccoli And Mushroom Egg Casserole 16
Couscous & Cucumber Bowl 16
Mango-yogurt Smoothie 16
Cherry Tomato & Mushroom Frittata 17
Avocado & Peach Power Smoothie 17
Za'atar Pizza 17
Easy Pizza Pockets 17
Zucchini & Tomato Cheese Tart 18
Tomato And Egg Breakfast Pizza 18
Zucchini Hummus Wraps 19
Mediterranean Omelet 19
Pesto Salami & Cheese Egg Cupcakes 19

Vegetable Mains And Meatless Recipes 20
Baked Potato With Veggie Mix 21
Roasted Artichokes 21
Balsamic Grilled Vegetables 21
Spinach & Lentil Stew 22
Eggplant Rolls In Tomato Sauce 22

- Zoodles With Beet Pesto 23
- Chickpea Lettuce Wraps With Celery 23
- Simple Broccoli With Yogurt Sauce 23
- Homemade Vegetarian Moussaka 24
- Spicy Kale With Almonds 24
- Tradicional Matchuba Green Beans 24
- Creamy Polenta With Mushrooms 25
- Parsley & Olive Zucchini Bake 25
- Baked Vegetable Stew 26
- Baked Honey Acorn Squash 26
- Grilled Eggplant "steaks" With Sauce 26
- Cauliflower Cakes With Goat Cheese 27
- Veggie-stuffed Portabello Mushrooms 27
- Mini Crustless Spinach Quiches 28
- Zucchini Crisp 28
- Spicy Roasted Tomatoes 29
- Minty Broccoli & Walnuts 29
- Moroccan Tagine With Vegetables 29
- Sweet Mustard Cabbage Hash 30
- Rainbow Vegetable Kebabs 30
- Parmesan Stuffed Zucchini Boats 30
- Simple Honey-glazed Baby Carrots 31
- Tasty Lentil Burgers 31

Fish And Seafood Recipes 32

- Parsley Littleneck Clams In Sherry Sauce 33
- Baked Oysters With Vegetables 33
- Roasted Red Snapper With Citrus Topping 34
- Spicy Cod Fillets 34
- Baked Anchovies With Chili-garlic Topping 34
- Shrimp & Salmon In Tomato Sauce 35
- Lemony Shrimp With Orzo Salad 35
- Fennel & Bell Pepper Salmon 36
- Mustard Sardine Cakes 36
- Salmon Stuffed Peppers 36
- Anchovy Spread With Avocado 36
- Salmon And Mushroom Hash With Pesto 37
- Baked Cod With Lemony Rice 37
- Spicy Haddock Stew 38
- Shrimp And Pea Paella 38
- Walnut-crusted Salmon 39
- Sicilian-style Squid With Zucchini 39
- Better-for-you Cod & Potatoes 39
- Seafood Stew 40
- Thyme Hake With Potatoes 40
- Lemon-parsley Swordfish 41
- Parsley Tomato Tilapia 41
- Wine-steamed Clams 41

Cod Fettuccine 41
Grilled Sardines With Herby Sauce 42
Easy Tomato Tuna Melts 42
Balsamic-honey Glazed Salmon 43
Salmon Packets 43

Poultry And Meats Recipes 44

Tangy Mushroom & Chicken Kabobs 45
Roasted Pork Tenderloin With Apple Sauce 45
Homemade Pizza Burgers 46
Chicken Drumsticks With Peach Glaze 46
Beef & Bell Pepper Bake 46
Marsala Chicken Cacciatore Stir-fry 47
Chicken Thighs Al Orange 47
Saucy Turkey With Ricotta Cheese 47
Beef Filet Mignon In Mushroom Sauce 48
Chicken Tagine With Vegetables 48
Pork Loaf With Colby Cheese 49
Beef & Pumpkin Stew 49
Greek-style Chicken & Vegetable Stir-fry 49
Eggplant & Turkey Moussaka 50
Roasted Herby Chicken 50
Tzatziki Chicken Loaf 50
Eggplant & Chicken Skillet 51
Chicken Sausages With Pepper Sauce 51
Herby Beef Soup 51
Beef, Tomato, And Lentils Stew 52
Pork Butt With Leeks 52
Easy Pork Souvlaki 52
Deluxe Chicken With Yogurt Sauce 53
Chicken Cacciatore 53
Grilled Chicken Breasts With Italian Sauce 53
Turmeric Green Bean & Chicken Bake 54
Asparagus & Chicken Skillet 54
Tender Pork Shoulder 54

Sides , Salads, And Soups Recipes 55

Sun-dried Tomato & Spinach Pasta Salad 56
Zesty Asparagus Salad 56
Cucumber & Tomato Salad With Anchovies 56
Moroccan Spinach & Lentil Soup 57
Orange-honey Glazed Carrots 57
Grilled Bell Pepper And Anchovy Antipasto 57
Classic Potato Salad With Green Onions 58
Tricolor Summer Salad 58
Brussels Sprout And Apple Slaw 58
Collard Green & Rice Salad 59

Zoodles With Tomato-mushroom Sauce ... 59
Italian Spinach & Rice Soup ... 59
Leek & Shrimp Soup ... 60
Mascarpone Sweet Potato Mash ... 60
Summer Gazpacho ... 60
Baby Spinach & Apple Salad With Walnuts ... 60
Greek Chicken, Tomato, And Olive Salad ... 61
Pine Nut & Raisin Spinach ... 61
Roasted Cherry Tomato & Fennel ... 61
Parsley Turkish Chicken Soup ... 62
Root Vegetable Roast ... 62
Mushroom And Soba Noodle Soup ... 62
Parmesan Roasted Red Potatoes ... 63
Classic Aioli ... 63
Eggplant Casserole With Pecorino Cheese ... 63
Rich Chicken And Small Pasta Broth ... 64
Pecorino Zucchini Strips ... 64
Green Beans With Tahini-lemon Sauce ... 64

Beans, Grains, And Pastas Recipes ... 65

Easy Walnut And Ricotta Spaghetti ... 66
Sweet Potatoes Stuffed With Beans ... 66
Raspberry & Nut Quinoa ... 67
Spinach Farfalle With Ricotta Cheese ... 67
Tomato Sauce And Basil Pesto Fettuccine ... 67
Paprika Spinach & Chickpea Bowl ... 68
Parmesan Beef Rotini With Asparagus ... 68
Cranberry & Walnut Freekeh Pilaf ... 68
Valencian-style Mussel Rice ... 69
Florentine Bean & Vegetable Gratin ... 69
Spanish-style Linguine With Tapenade ... 69
Green Pea & Cavolo Nero Farro Pilaf ... 70
Bolognese Penne Bake ... 70
Ricotta & Olive Rigatoni ... 70
Kale Chicken With Pappardelle ... 71
Caprese Pasta With Roasted Asparagus ... 71
Traditional Beef Lasagna ... 72
Cherry, Apricot, And Pecan Brown Rice Bowl ... 72
Carrot & Caper Chickpeas ... 73
Two-bean Cassoulet ... 73
Parmesan Zucchini Farfalle ... 73
Freekeh Pilaf With Dates And Pistachios ... 74
Lebanese Flavor Broken Thin Noodles ... 74
Sun-dried Tomato & Basil Risotto ... 75
Roasted Pepper Brown Rice ... 75
Authentic Fettuccine A La Puttanesca ... 75
Kale & Feta Couscous ... 76
Roasted Ratatouille Pasta ... 76

Fruits, Desserts And Snacks Recipes 77
Spicy Hummus 78
Pepperoni Fat Head Pizza 78
Portuguese Orange Mug Cake 79
Stuffed Cherry Tomatoes 79
Baked Balsamic Beet Rounds 79
Chili Grilled Eggplant Rounds 79
Crunchy Almond Cookies 80
Fancy Baileys Ice Coffee 80
Mascarpone Baked Pears 80
Salt & Pepper Toasted Walnuts 81
The Best Anchovy Tapenade 81
Spicy Chorizo Pizza 81
Quick & Easy Red Dip 82
Mini Cucumber & Cream Cheese Sandwiches 82
Grilled Peaches With Whipped Ricotta 82
Simple Apple Compote 83
Energy Granola Bites 83
Ultimate Seed Crackers 83
Berry And Rhubarb Cobbler 84
Parsley Lamb Arancini 84
Chickpea & Spinach Salad With Almonds 85
Easy Blueberry And Oat Crisp 85
Rice Pudding With Roasted Orange 85
Orange Pannacotta With Blackberries 86
Skillet Pesto Pizza 86
Fruit Skewers With Vanilla Labneh 86
Charred Maple Pineapple 87
Lebanese Spicy Baba Ganoush 87

30 Day Meal Plan 88

Appendix : Recipes Index 90

INTRODUCTION

My name is Tabatha Coughlin and I am the author of the Mediterranean Diet Cookbook. I was diagnosed with a heart condition a few years ago and was told that I needed to make some lifestyle changes in order to improve my health. After doing some research, I discovered the Mediterranean Diet and decided to give it a try. I was amazed at how quickly I began to feel better and I was inspired to share the benefits of this way of eating with others. That's why I wrote the Mediterranean Diet Cookbook.

The Mediterranean Diet Cookbook is the perfect guide for anyone looking to make the switch to a healthier lifestyle. This book contains over 1800 delicious recipes, as well as a 28-day meal plan to help you get started.

It also includes information about the health benefits of the Mediterranean Diet, as well as tips and tricks for making the most of this way of eating.

With the help of this cookbook, you can learn about this healthy way of eating and enjoy delicious, nutritious meals. The recipes are easy to follow and are designed to help you get the most out of the Mediterranean Diet. Whether you are looking to lose weight, improve your overall health, or just enjoy delicious meals, this cookbook has something for everyone.

With the help of the Mediterranean Diet Cookbook, you can make the switch to a healthier lifestyle and enjoy the benefits of the Mediterranean Diet. Now, enjoy the delicious recipes together!

What exactly is the Mediterranean Diet?

The Mediterranean Diet is a way of eating that is based on the traditional diets of countries around the Mediterranean Sea. It emphasizes the consumption of fresh fruits and vegetables, whole grains, legumes, nuts, and healthy fats such as olive oil. It also includes moderate amounts of fish, poultry, and dairy.

This diet is known for its health benefits, including reducing the risk of heart disease, diabetes, and obesity.

What are the benefits of the Mediterranean Diet?

The Mediterranean Diet has many health benefits, including reducing the risk of heart disease, diabetes, and obesity. It is also associated with improved cognitive function, better mental health, and a lower risk of certain types of cancer.

Additionally, the Mediterranean Diet is rich in antioxidants, which can help protect against oxidative stress and inflammation. This diet is also known for its anti-aging benefits, as it can help reduce the signs of aging and improve overall health.

How to get started with a Mediterranean Diet?

Starting a Mediterranean Diet with the 1800 Recipes Mediterranean Diet Cookbook is a great way to get started.

Begin by reading through the recipes and selecting ones that you would like to try. Make sure to include a variety of fresh fruits and vegetables, whole grains, legumes, nuts, and healthy fats such as olive oil.

Additionally, include moderate amounts of fish, poultry, and dairy. Limit processed foods and sugar, as well as red meat and saturated fats.

Finally, stay active and get plenty of exercise. With these simple steps, you can start to enjoy the health benefits of the Mediterranean Diet.

Measurement Conversions

BASIC KITCHEN CONVERSIONS & EQUIVALENTS

DRY MEASUREMENTS CONVERSION CHART

3 TEASPOONS = 1 TABLESPOON = 1/16 CUP

6 TEASPOONS = 2 TABLESPOONS = 1/8 CUP

12 TEASPOONS = 4 TABLESPOONS = 1/4 CUP

24 TEASPOONS = 8 TABLESPOONS = 1/2 CUP

36 TEASPOONS = 12 TABLESPOONS = 3/4 CUP

48 TEASPOONS = 16 TABLESPOONS = 1 CUP

METRIC TO US COOKING CONVERSIONS

OVEN TEMPERATURES

120 °C = 250 °F

160 °C = 320 °F

180° C = 350 °F

205 °C = 400 °F

220 °C = 425 °F

LIQUID MEASUREMENTS CONVERSION CHART

8 FLUID OUNCES = 1 CUP = 1/2 PINT = 1/4 QUART

16 FLUID OUNCES = 2 CUPS = 1 PINT = 1/2 QUART

32 FLUID OUNCES = 4 CUPS = 2 PINTS = 1 QUART = 1/4 GALLON

128 FLUID OUNCES = 16 CUPS = 8 PINTS = 4 QUARTS = 1 GALLON

BAKING IN GRAMS

1 CUP FLOUR = 140 GRAMS

1 CUP SUGAR = 150 GRAMS

1 CUP POWDERED SUGAR = 160 GRAMS

1 CUP HEAVY CREAM = 235 GRAMS

VOLUME

1 MILLILITER = 1/5 TEASPOON

5 ML = 1 TEASPOON

15 ML = 1 TABLESPOON

240 ML = 1 CUP OR 8 FLUID OUNCES

1 LITER = 34 FL. OUNCES

WEIGHT

1 GRAM = .035 OUNCES

100 GRAMS = 3.5 OUNCES

500 GRAMS = 1.1 POUNDS

1 KILOGRAM = 35 OUNCES

US TO METRIC COOKING CONVERSIONS

1/5 TSP = 1 ML

1 TSP = 5 ML

1 TBSP = 15 ML

1 FL OUNCE = 30 ML

1 CUP = 237 ML

1 PINT (2 CUPS) = 473 ML

1 QUART (4 CUPS) = .95 LITER

1 GALLON (16 CUPS) = 3.8 LITERS

1 OZ = 28 GRAMS

1 POUND = 454 GRAMS

BUTTER

1 CUP BUTTER = 2 STICKS = 8 OUNCES = 230 GRAMS = 8 TABLESPOONS

WHAT DOES 1 CUP EQUAL

1 CUP = 8 FLUID OUNCES

1 CUP = 16 TABLESPOONS

1 CUP = 48 TEASPOONS

1 CUP = 1/2 PINT

1 CUP = 1/4 QUART

1 CUP = 1/16 GALLON

1 CUP = 240 ML

BAKING PAN CONVERSIONS

1 CUP ALL-PURPOSE FLOUR = 4.5 OZ

1 CUP ROLLED OATS = 3 OZ 1 LARGE EGG = 1.7 OZ

1 CUP BUTTER = 8 OZ 1 CUP MILK = 8 OZ

1 CUP HEAVY CREAM = 8.4 OZ

1 CUP GRANULATED SUGAR = 7.1 OZ

1 CUP PACKED BROWN SUGAR = 7.75 OZ

1 CUP VEGETABLE OIL = 7.7 OZ

1 CUP UNSIFTED POWDERED SUGAR = 4.4 OZ

BAKING PAN CONVERSIONS

9-INCH ROUND CAKE PAN = 12 CUPS

10-INCH TUBE PAN = 16 CUPS

11-INCH BUNDT PAN = 12 CUPS

9-INCH SPRINGFORM PAN = 10 CUPS

9 X 5 INCH LOAF PAN = 8 CUPS

9-INCH SQUARE PAN = 8 CUPS

Breakfast Recipes Recipes

Breakfast Recipes Recipes

Feta & Olive Breakfast

Servings:4 | Cooking Time:15 Minutes

Ingredients:
- ¼ cup extra-virgin olive oil
- 4 feta cheese squares
- 3 cups mixed olives, drained
- 3 tbsp lemon juice
- 1 tsp lemon zest
- 1 tsp dried dill
- Pita bread for serving

Directions:

1. In a small bowl, whisk together the olive oil, lemon juice, lemon zest, and dill. Place the feta cheese on a serving plate and add the mixed olives. Pour the dressing all over the feta cheese. Serve with toasted pita bread.

Nutrition Info:
- Per Serving: Calories: 406;Fat: 38.2g;Protein: 7.9g;Carbs: 8g.

Classic Shakshuka

Servings:2 | Cooking Time: 30 Minutes

Ingredients:
- 1 tablespoon olive oil
- ½ red pepper, diced
- ½ medium onion, diced
- 2 small garlic cloves, minced
- ½ teaspoon smoked paprika
- ½ teaspoon cumin
- Pinch red pepper flakes
- 1 can fire-roasted tomatoes
- ¼ teaspoon salt
- Pinch freshly ground black pepper
- 1 ounce crumbled feta cheese (about ¼ cup)
- 3 large eggs
- 3 tablespoons minced fresh parsley

Directions:

1. Heat the olive oil in a skillet over medium-high heat and add the pepper, onion, and garlic. Sauté until the vegetables start to turn golden.
2. Add the paprika, cumin, and red pepper flakes and stir to toast the spices for about 30 seconds. Add the tomatoes with their juices.
3. Reduce the heat and let the sauce simmer for 10 minutes, or until it starts to thicken. Add the salt and pepper. Taste the sauce and adjust seasonings as necessary.
4. Scatter the feta cheese on top. Make 3 wells in the sauce and crack one egg into each well.
5. Cover and let the eggs cook for about 7 minutes. Remove the lid and continue cooking for 5 minutes more, or until the yolks are cooked to desired doneness.
6. Garnish with fresh parsley and serve.

Nutrition Info:
- Per Serving: Calories: 289;Fat: 18.2g;Protein: 15.1g;Carbs: 18.5g.

Yummy Lentil Stuffed Pitas

Servings:4 | Cooking Time:20 Minutes

Ingredients:
- 4 pitta breads, halved horizontally
- 2 tbsp olive oil
- 1 tomato, cubed
- 1 red onion, chopped
- 1 garlic clove, minced
- ¼ cup parsley, chopped
- 1 cup lentils, rinsed
- ¼ cup lemon juice
- Salt and black pepper to taste

Directions:

1. Bring a pot of salted water to a boil over high heat. Pour in the lentils and lower the heat. Cover and let it simmer for 15 minutes or until lentils are tender, adding more water if needed. Drain and set aside.
2. Warm the olive oil in a skillet over medium heat and cook the onion and garlic and for 3 minutes until soft and translucent. Stir in tomato, lemon juice, salt, and pepper and cook for another 10 minutes. Add the lentils and parsley to the skillet and stir to combine. Fill the pita bread with the lentil mixture. Roll up and serve immediately. Enjoy!

Nutrition Info:
- Per Serving: Calories: 390;Fat: 2g;Protein: 29g;Carbs: 68g.

Veg Mix And Blackeye Pea Burritos

Servings: 6 | Cooking Time: 40 Minutes

Ingredients:

- 1 teaspoon olive oil
- 1 red onion, diced
- 2 garlic cloves, minced
- 1 zucchini, chopped
- 1 tomato, diced
- 1 bell pepper, any color, deseeded and diced
- 1 can blackeye peas
- 2 teaspoons chili powder
- Sea salt, to taste
- 6 whole-grain tortillas

Directions:

1. Preheat the oven to 325°F.
2. Heat the olive oil in a nonstick skillet over medium heat or until shimmering.
3. Add the onion and sauté for 5 minutes or until translucent.
4. Add the garlic and sauté for 30 seconds or until fragrant.
5. Add the zucchini and sauté for 5 minutes or until tender.
6. Add the tomato and bell pepper and sauté for 2 minutes or until soft.
7. Fold in the black peas and sprinkle them with chili powder and salt. Stir to mix well.
8. Place the tortillas on a clean work surface, then top them with sautéed vegetables mix.
9. Fold one ends of tortillas over the vegetable mix, then tuck and roll them into burritos.
10. Arrange the burritos in a baking dish, seam side down, then pour the juice remains in the skillet over the burritos.
11. Bake in the preheated oven for 25 minutes or until golden brown.
12. Serve immediately.

Nutrition Info:

- Per Serving: Calories: 335;Fat: 16.2g;Protein: 12.1g;Carbs: 8.3g.

Baked Eggs In Avocado

Servings: 2 | Cooking Time: 10 To 15 Minutes

Ingredients:

- 1 ripe large avocado
- 2 large eggs
- Salt and freshly ground black pepper, to taste
- 4 tablespoons jarred pesto, for serving
- 2 tablespoons chopped tomato, for serving
- 2 tablespoons crumbled feta cheese, for serving (optional)

Directions:

1. Preheat the oven to 425°F.
2. Slice the avocado in half, remove the pit and scoop out a generous tablespoon of flesh from each half to create a hole big enough to fit an egg.
3. Transfer the avocado halves (cut-side up) to a baking sheet.
4. Crack 1 egg into each avocado half and sprinkle with salt and pepper.
5. Bake in the preheated oven for 10 to 15 minutes, or until the eggs are cooked to your preferred doneness.
6. Remove the avocado halves from the oven. Scatter each avocado half evenly with the jarred pesto, chopped tomato, and crumbled feta cheese (if desired). Serve immediately.

Nutrition Info:

- Per Serving: Calories: 301;Fat: 25.9g;Protein: 8.1g;Carbs: 9.8g.

Red Pepper Coques With Pine Nuts

Servings: 4 | Cooking Time: 45 Minutes

Ingredients:
- Dough:
- 3 cups almond flour
- ½ teaspoon instant or rapid-rise yeast
- 2 teaspoons raw honey
- 1⅓ cups ice water
- 3 tablespoons extra-virgin olive oil
- 1½ teaspoons sea salt
- Red Pepper Topping:
- 4 tablespoons extra-virgin olive oil, divided
- 2 cups jarred roasted red peppers, patted dry and sliced thinly
- 2 large onions, halved and sliced thin
- 3 garlic cloves, minced
- ¼ teaspoon red pepper flakes
- 2 bay leaves
- 3 tablespoons maple syrup
- 1½ teaspoons sea salt
- 3 tablespoons red whine vinegar
- For Garnish:
- ¼ cup pine nuts (optional)
- 1 tablespoon minced fresh parsley

Directions:
1. Make the Dough:
2. Combine the flour, yeast, and honey in a food processor, pulse to combine well. Gently add water while pulsing. Let the dough sit for 10 minutes.
3. Mix the olive oil and salt in the dough and knead the dough until smooth. Wrap in plastic and refrigerate for at least 1 day.
4. Make the Topping:
5. Heat 1 tablespoon of olive oil in a nonstick skillet over medium heat until shimmering.
6. Add the red peppers, onions, garlic, red pepper flakes, bay leaves, maple syrup, and salt. Sauté for 20 minutes or until the onion is caramelized.
7. Turn off the heat and discard the bay leaves. Remove the onion from the skillet and baste with wine vinegar. Let them sit until ready to use.
8. Make the Coques:
9. Preheat the oven to 500ºF. Grease two baking sheets with 1 tablespoon of olive oil.
10. Divide the dough ball into four balls, then press and shape them into equal-sized oval. Arrange the ovals on the baking sheets and pierce each dough about 12 times.
11. Rub the ovals with 2 tablespoons of olive oil and bake for 7 minutes or until puffed. Flip the ovals halfway through the cooking time.
12. Spread the ovals with the topping and pine nuts, then bake for an additional 15 minutes or until well browned.
13. Remove the coques from the oven and spread with parsley. Allow to cool for 10 minutes before serving.

Nutrition Info:
- Per Serving: Calories: 658;Fat: 23.1g;Protein: 3.4g;Carbs: 112.0g.

Morning Pizza Frittata

Servings: 4 | Cooking Time: 20 Minutes

Ingredients:
- 2 tbsp butter
- 8 oz pancetta, chopped
- ½ onion, finely chopped
- 1 cup mushrooms, sliced
- 8 large eggs, beaten
- ¼ cup heavy cream
- 1 tsp dried oregano
- ¼ tsp red pepper flakes
- ½ cup mozzarella, shredded
- 8 cherry tomatoes, halved
- 4 black olives, sliced

Directions:
1. Melt the butter in a large skillet over medium heat until. Add the pancetta and cook for 4 minutes until browned. Stir in the onion and mushrooms and cook for 3 more minutes, stirring occasionally, until the veggies are tender. In a bowl, beat the eggs, heavy cream, oregano, and red pepper flakes.
2. Pour over the veggies and pancetta. Cook for about 5-6 minutes until the eggs are set. Spread the mozzarella cheese all over and arrange the cherry tomatoes on top. Place under the preheated broiler for 4-5 minutes. Leave to cool slightly and cut into wedges. Top with sliced olives and serve warm.

Nutrition Info:
- Per Serving: Calories: 595;Fat: 43g;Protein: 38g;Carbs: 14g.

Mushroom And Caramelized Onion Musakhan

Servings: 4 | Cooking Time: 1 Hour 5 Minutes

Ingredients:
- 2 tablespoons sumac, plus more for sprinkling
- 1 teaspoon ground allspice
- ½ teaspoon ground cardamom
- ½ teaspoon ground cumin
- 3 tablespoons extra-virgin olive oil, divided
- 2 pounds portobello mushroom caps, gills removed, caps halved and sliced ½ inch thick
- 3 medium white onions, coarsely chopped
- ¼ cup water
- Kosher salt, to taste
- 1 whole-wheat Turkish flatbread
- ¼ cup pine nuts
- 1 lemon, wedged

Directions:
1. Preheat the oven to 350ºF.
2. Combine 2 tablespoons of sumac, allspice, cardamom, and cumin in a small bowl. Stir to mix well.
3. Heat 2 tablespoons of olive oil in an oven-proof skillet over medium-high heat until shimmering.
4. Add the mushroom to the skillet and sprinkle with half of sumac mixture. Sauté for 8 minutes or until the mushrooms are tender. You may need to work in batches to avoid overcrowding. Transfer the mushrooms to a plate and set side.
5. Heat 1 tablespoon of olive oil in the skillet over medium-high heat until shimmering.
6. Add the onion and sauté for 20 minutes or until caramelized. Sprinkle with remaining sumac mixture, then cook for 1 more minute.
7. Pour in the water and sprinkle with salt. Bring to a simmer.
8. Turn off the heat and put the mushroom back to the skillet.
9. Place the skillet in the preheated oven and bake for 30 minutes.
10. Remove the skillet from the oven and let the mushroom sit for 10 minutes until cooled down.
11. Heat the Turkish flatbread in a baking dish in the oven for 5 minutes or until warmed through.
12. Arrange the bread on a large plate and top with mushrooms, onions, and roasted pine nuts. Squeeze the lemon wedges over and sprinkle with more sumac. Serve immediately.

Nutrition Info:
- Per Serving: Calories: 336;Fat: 18.7g;Protein: 11.5g;Carbs: 34.3g.

Tomato Eggs With Fried Potatoes

Servings: 2 | Cooking Time: 20 Minutes

Ingredients:
- 2 tbsp + ½ cup olive oil
- 3 medium tomatoes, puréed
- 1 tbsp fresh tarragon, chopped
- 1 garlic clove, minced
- Salt and black pepper to taste
- 3 potatoes, cubed
- 4 fresh eggs
- 1 tsp fresh oregano, chopped

Directions:
1. Warm 2 tbsp of olive oil in a saucepan over medium heat. Add the garlic and sauté for 1 minute. Pour in the tomatoes, tarragon, salt, and pepper. Reduce the heat and cook for 5-8 minutes or until the sauce is thickened and bubbly.
2. Warm the remaining olive oil in a skillet over medium heat. Fry the potatoes for 5 minutes until crisp and browned on the outside, then cover and reduce heat to low. Steam potatoes until done. Carefully crack the eggs into the tomato sauce.
3. Cook over low heat until the eggs are set in the sauce, about 6 minutes. Remove the potatoes from the pan, drain them on paper towels, and place them in a bowl. Sprinkle with salt and pepper and top with oregano. Carefully remove the eggs with a slotted spoon and place them on a plate with the potatoes. Spoon sauce over and serve.

Nutrition Info:
- Per Serving: Calories: 1146;Fat: 69g;Protein: 26g;-Carbs: 45g.

Hot Zucchini & Egg Nests

Servings:4 | Cooking Time:25 Minutes

Ingredients:
- 2 tbsp olive oil
- 4 eggs
- 1 lb zucchinis, shredded
- Salt and black pepper to taste
- ½ red chili pepper, minced
- 2 tbsp parsley, chopped

Directions:
1. Preheat the oven to 360 °F. Combine zucchini, salt, pepper, and olive oil in a bowl. Form nest shapes with a spoon onto a greased baking sheet. Crack an egg into each nest and season with salt, pepper, and chili pepper. Bake for 11 minutes. Serve topped with parsley.

Nutrition Info:
- Per Serving: Calories: 141;Fat: 11.6g;Protein: 7g;-Carbs: 4.2g.

Citrus French Toasts

Servings:4 | Cooking Time:30 Minutes

Ingredients:
- 1 tbsp butter
- 1 orange, juiced and zested
- 4 bread slices
- 1 ½ cups milk
- 2 eggs, beaten
- 1 tsp vanilla extract
- 1 tsp ground cinnamon
- 1 tbsp powdered sugar

Directions:
1. Beat milk, eggs, vanilla, orange zest, and orange juice in a bowl. Lay the bread in a rectangular baking dish in an even layer. Cover with the egg mixture and let it stand for 10 minutes, flipping once, to absorb well.
2. Melt the butter in a skillet over medium heat and fry the bread in batches until golden brown on both sides, about 6-8 minutes. Dust with powdered sugar and cinnamon. Serve.

Nutrition Info:
- Per Serving: Calories: 160;Fat: 7.3g;Protein: 6.9g;-Carbs: 17g.

Basil Cheese Omelet

Servings:2 | Cooking Time:20 Minutes

Ingredients:
- 1 tbsp olive oil
- ½ pint cherry tomatoes
- 2 garlic cloves, minced
- 5 large eggs, beaten
- 3 tbsp milk
- Salt and black pepper to taste
- 2 tbsp fresh oregano, minced
- 2 tbsp fresh basil, minced
- 2 oz ricotta cheese, crumbled

Directions:
1. Warm the olive oil in a skillet over medium heat. Add the cherry tomatoes. Reduce the heat, cover the pan, and let the tomatoes soften. When the tomatoes are mostly softened and broken down, remove the lid, add garlic and continue to sauté.
2. In a bowl, combine the eggs, milk, salt, pepper, and herbs and whisk well to combine. Increase the heat to medium, pour the egg mixture over the tomatoes and garlic, and then sprinkle with ricotta cheese. Cook for 7-8 minutes, flipping once until the eggs are set. Run a spatula around the edge of the pan to make sure they won't stick. Serve warm.

Nutrition Info:
- Per Serving: Calories: 394;Fat: 29.6g;Protein: 26g;-Carbs: 6g.

Lemon Cardamom Buckwheat Pancakes

Servings:2 | Cooking Time:20 Minutes

Ingredients:

- ½ cup buckwheat flour
- ½ tsp cardamom
- ½ tsp baking powder
- ½ cup milk
- ¼ cup plain Greek yogurt
- 1 egg
- 1 tsp lemon zest
- 1 tbsp honey

Directions:

1. Mix the buckwheat flour, cardamom, and baking powder in a medium bowl. Whisk the milk, yogurt, egg, lemon zest, and honey in another bowl. Add the wet ingredients to the dry ingredients and stir until the batter is smooth.

2. Spray a frying pan with non-stick cooking oil and cook the pancakes over medium heat until the edges begin to brown. Flip and cook on the other side for 3 more minutes. Serve.

Nutrition Info:

- Per Serving: Calories: 196;Fat: 6g;Protein: 10g;-Carbs: 27g.

Strawberry Basil Mascarpone Toast

Servings:2 | Cooking Time:15 Minutes

Ingredients:

- 4 fresh basil leaves, sliced into thin shreds
- 4 whole-grain bread slices, toasted
- ½ cup mascarpone cheese
- 1 tbsp honey
- 1 cup strawberries, sliced

Directions:

1. In a small bowl, combine the mascarpone and honey. Spread the mixture evenly over each slice of bread. Top with sliced strawberries and basil.

Nutrition Info:

- Per Serving: Calories: 275;Fat: 8g;Protein: 16g;-Carbs: 41g.

Berry-yogurt Smoothie

Servings:1 | Cooking Time:5 Minutes

Ingredients:

- ½ cup Greek yogurt
- ¼ cup milk
- ½ cup fresh blueberries
- 1 tsp vanilla sugar
- 2 ice cubes

Directions:

1. Pulse the Greek yogurt, milk, vanilla sugar, and berries in your blender until the berries are liquefied. Add the ice cubes and blend on high until thick and smooth. Serve.

Nutrition Info:

- Per Serving: Calories: 230;Fat: 8.8g;Protein: 16g;-Carbs: 23g.

Chocolate-strawberry Smoothie

Servings:2 | Cooking Time:5 Minutes

Ingredients:

- 1 cup buttermilk
- 2 cups strawberries, hulled
- 1 cup crushed ice
- 3 tbsp cocoa powder
- 3 tbsp honey
- 2 mint leaves

Directions:

1. In a food processor, pulse buttermilk, strawberries, ice, cocoa powder, mint, and honey until smooth. Serve.

Nutrition Info:

- Per Serving: Calories: 209;Fat: 2.6g;Protein: 7g;-Carbs: 47.2g.

Cheesy Broccoli And Mushroom Egg Casserole

Servings:4 | Cooking Time: 40 Minutes

Ingredients:

- 2 tablespoons extra-virgin olive oil
- ½ sweet onion, chopped
- 1 teaspoon minced garlic
- 1 cup sliced button mushrooms
- 1 cup chopped broccoli
- 8 large eggs
- ¼ cup unsweetened almond milk
- 1 tablespoon chopped fresh basil
- 1 cup shredded Cheddar cheese
- Sea salt and freshly ground black pepper, to taste

Directions:

1. Preheat the oven to 375ºF.
2. Heat the olive oil in a large ovenproof skillet over medium-high heat.
3. Add the onion, garlic, and mushrooms to the skillet and sauté for about 5 minutes, stirring occasionally.
4. Stir in the broccoli and sauté for 5 minutes until the vegetables start to soften.
5. Meanwhile, beat the eggs with the almond milk and basil in a small bowl until well mixed.
6. Remove the skillet from the heat and pour the egg mixture over the top. Scatter the Cheddar cheese all over.
7. Bake uncovered in the preheated oven for about 30 minutes, or until the top of the casserole is golden brown and a fork inserted in the center comes out clean.
8. Remove from the oven and sprinkle with the sea salt and pepper. Serve hot.

Nutrition Info:

- Per Serving: Calories: 326;Fat: 27.2g;Protein: 14.1g;Carbs: 6.7g.

Couscous & Cucumber Bowl

Servings:4 | Cooking Time:15 Minutes

Ingredients:

- 2 tbsp olive oil
- ¾ cup couscous
- 1 cup water
- 1 yellow onion, chopped
- 2 garlic cloves, minced
- 2 cups canned chickpeas
- Salt to taste
- 15 oz canned tomatoes, diced
- 1 cucumber, cut into ribbons
- ½ cup black olives, chopped
- 1 tbsp lemon juice
- 1 tbsp mint leaves, chopped

Directions:

1. Cover the couscous with salted boiling water, cover, and let it sit for about 5 minutes. Then fluff with a fork and set aside.
2. Warm the olive oil in a skillet over medium heat and sauté onion and garlic for 3 minutes until soft. Stir in chickpeas, salt, and tomatoes for 1-2 minutes. Turn off the heat and mix in olives, couscous, and lemon juice. Transfer to a bowl and top with cucumber ribbons and mint to serve.

Nutrition Info:

- Per Serving: Calories: 350;Fat: 11g;Protein: 12g;Carbs: 50g.

Mango-yogurt Smoothie

Servings:2 | Cooking Time:5 Minutes

Ingredients:

- 6 oz Greek yogurt
- 2 mangoes, chopped
- 2 tbsp milk
- 7-8 ice cubes

Directions:

1. In a food processor, place the mango, milk, yogurt, and ice cubes. Pulse until creamy and smooth. Serve right away.

Nutrition Info:

- Per Serving: Calories: 261;Fat: 2g;Protein: 12g;Carbs: 54g.

Cherry Tomato & Mushroom Frittata

Servings:4 | Cooking Time:30 Minutes

Ingredients:
- 1 cup Italian brown mushrooms, sliced
- 2 tbsp olive oil
- 2 spring onions, chopped
- 8 cherry tomatoes, halved
- 6 eggs
- ½ cup milk
- Salt and black pepper to taste
- ¼ cup grated Parmesan
- ½ tbsp Italian seasoning mix

Directions:

1. Preheat oven to 370 F. Mix eggs, milk, Italian seasoning, salt, and pepper in a bowl. Warm olive oil in a skillet over medium heat until sizzling. Add in mushrooms, spring onions, and tomatoes and sauté for 5 minutes.
2. Pour in the egg mixture and cook for 5 minutes until the eggs are set. Scatter Parmesan cheese and bake in the oven for 6-7 minutes until the cheese melts. Slice before serving.

Nutrition Info:
- Per Serving: Calories: 227;Fat: 15g;Protein: 13g;-Carbs: 13g.

Avocado & Peach Power Smoothie

Servings:2 | Cooking Time:10 Minutes

Ingredients:
- 1 tbsp sesame seeds
- 1 tsp sugar
- 2 peaches, cored and chopped
- ½ cup Greek yogurt
- ½ ripe avocado, chopped
- 2 tbsp flax meal
- 1 tsp vanilla extract
- 1 tsp orange extract

Directions:

1. Blend the sesame seeds, sugar, peaches, yogurt, avocado, flax meal, vanilla, orange extract, and honey in your food processor until smooth. Pour the mixture into 2 bowls. Serve.

Nutrition Info:
- Per Serving: Calories: 213;Fat: 13g;Protein: 6g;-Carbs: 23g.

Za'atar Pizza

Servings:4 | Cooking Time: 1o To 12 Minutes

Ingredients:
- 1 sheet puff pastry
- ¼ cup extra-virgin olive oil
- ⅓ cup za'atar seasoning

Directions:

1. Preheat the oven to 350ºF. Line a baking sheet with parchment paper.
2. Place the puff pastry on the prepared baking sheet. Cut the pastry into desired slices.
3. Brush the pastry with the olive oil. Sprinkle with the za'atar seasoning.
4. Put the pastry in the oven and bake for 10 to 12 minutes, or until edges are lightly browned and puffed up.
5. Serve warm.

Nutrition Info:
- Per Serving: Calories: 374;Fat: 30.0g;Protein: 3.0g;-Carbs: 20.0g.

Easy Pizza Pockets

Servings:2 | Cooking Time: 0 Minutes

Ingredients:
- ½ cup tomato sauce
- ½ teaspoon oregano
- ½ teaspoon garlic powder
- ½ cup chopped black olives
- 2 canned artichoke hearts, drained and chopped
- 2 ounces pepperoni, chopped
- ½ cup shredded Mozzarella cheese
- 1 whole-wheat pita, halved

Directions:

1. In a medium bowl, stir together the tomato sauce, oregano, and garlic powder.
2. Add the olives, artichoke hearts, pepperoni, and cheese. Stir to mix.
3. Spoon the mixture into the pita halves and serve.

Nutrition Info:
- Per Serving: Calories: 375;Fat: 23.5g;Protein: 17.1g;Carbs: 27.1g.

Zucchini & Tomato Cheese Tart

Servings: 6 | Cooking Time: 60 Minutes

Ingredients:
- 3 tbsp olive oil
- 5 sun-dried tomatoes, chopped
- 1 prepared pie crust
- 1 onion, chopped
- 2 garlic cloves, minced
- 2 zucchinis, chopped
- 1 red bell pepper, chopped
- 6 Kalamata olives, sliced
- 1 tsp fresh dill, chopped
- ½ cup Greek yogurt
- 1 cup feta cheese, crumbled
- 4 eggs
- 1 ½ cups milk
- Salt and black pepper to taste

Directions:

1. Preheat the oven to 380°F. Warm the olive oil in a skillet over medium heat and sauté garlic and onion for 3 minutes. Add in bell pepper and zucchini and sauté for another 3 minutes. Stir in olives, dill, salt, and pepper for 1-2 minutes and add tomatoes and feta cheese. Mix well and turn the heat off.

2. Press the crust gently into a lightly greased pie dish and prick it with a fork. Bake in the oven for 10-15 minutes until pale gold. Spread the zucchini mixture over the pie crust. Whisk the eggs with salt, pepper, milk, and yogurt in a bowl, then pour over the zucchini layer. Bake for 25-30 minutes until golden brown. Let cool before serving.

Nutrition Info:
- Per Serving: Calories: 220;Fat: 16g;Protein: 10g;-Carbs: 14g.

Tomato And Egg Breakfast Pizza

Servings: 2 | Cooking Time: 15 Minutes

Ingredients:
- 2 slices of whole-wheat naan bread
- 2 tablespoons prepared pesto
- 1 medium tomato, sliced
- 2 large eggs

Directions:

1. Heat a large nonstick skillet over medium-high heat. Place the naan bread in the skillet and let warm for about 2 minutes on each side, or until softened.

2. Spread 1 tablespoon of the pesto on one side of each slice and top with tomato slices.

3. Remove from the skillet and place each one on its own plate.

4. Crack the eggs into the skillet, keeping them separated, and cook until the whites are no longer translucent and the yolk is cooked to desired doneness.

5. Using a spatula, spoon one egg onto each bread slice. Serve warm.

Nutrition Info:
- Per Serving: Calories: 429;Fat: 16.8g;Protein: 18.1g;Carbs: 12.0g.

Zucchini Hummus Wraps

Servings: 2 | Cooking Time: 6 Minutes

Ingredients:
- 1 zucchini, ends removed, thinly sliced lengthwise
- ½ teaspoon dried oregano
- ¼ teaspoon freshly ground black pepper
- ¼ teaspoon garlic powder
- ¼ cup hummus
- 2 whole wheat tortillas
- 2 Roma tomatoes, cut lengthwise into slices
- 1 cup chopped kale
- 2 tablespoons chopped red onion
- ½ teaspoon ground cumin

Directions:

1. In a skillet over medium heat, place the zucchini slices and cook for 3 minutes per side. Sprinkle with the oregano, pepper, and garlic powder and remove from the heat.
2. Spread 2 tablespoons of hummus on each tortilla. Lay half the zucchini in the center of each tortilla. Top with tomato slices, kale, red onion, and ¼ teaspoon of cumin. Wrap tightly and serve.

Nutrition Info:
- Per Serving: Calories: 248; Fat: 8.1g; Protein: 9.1g; Carbs: 37.1g.

Mediterranean Omelet

Servings: 2 | Cooking Time: 15 Minutes

Ingredients:
- 2 teaspoons extra-virgin olive oil, divided
- 1 garlic clove, minced
- ½ yellow bell pepper, thinly sliced
- ½ red bell pepper, thinly sliced
- ¼ cup thinly sliced red onion
- 2 tablespoons chopped fresh parsley, plus extra for garnish
- 2 tablespoons chopped fresh basil
- ½ teaspoon salt
- ½ teaspoon freshly ground black pepper
- 4 large eggs, beaten

Directions:

1. In a large, heavy skillet, heat 1 teaspoon of the olive oil over medium heat. Add the garlic, peppers, and onion to the skillet and sauté, stirring frequently, for 5 minutes.
2. Add the parsley, basil, salt, and pepper, increase the heat to medium-high, and sauté for 2 minutes. Slide the vegetable mixture onto a plate and return the skillet to the heat.
3. Heat the remaining 1 teaspoon of olive oil in the skillet and pour in the beaten eggs, tilting the pan to coat evenly. Cook the eggs just until the edges are bubbly and all but the center is dry, 3 to 5 minutes.
4. Spoon the vegetable mixture onto one-half of the omelet and use a spatula to fold the empty side over the top. Slide the omelet onto a platter or cutting board.
5. To serve, cut the omelet in half and garnish with extra fresh parsley.

Nutrition Info:
- Per Serving: Calories: 206; Fat: 14.2g; Protein: 13.7g; Carbs: 7.2g.

Pesto Salami & Cheese Egg Cupcakes

Servings: 6 | Cooking Time: 25 Minutes

Ingredients:
- ½ cup roasted red peppers, chopped
- 1 tbsp olive oil
- 5 eggs, whisked
- 4 oz Italian dry salami, sliced
- 1/3 cup spinach, chopped
- ¼ cup ricotta cheese, crumbled
- Salt and black pepper to taste
- 1 ½ tbsp basil pesto

Directions:

1. Preheat the oven to 380 °F. Brush 6 ramekin cups with olive oil and line them with dry salami slices. Top with spinach, ricotta cheese, and roasted peppers. Whisk the eggs with pesto, salt, and pepper in a bowl and pour over the peppers. Bake for 15 minutes and serve warm.

Nutrition Info:
- Per Serving: Calories: 120; Fat: 8g; Protein: 10g; Carbs: 2g.

Vegetable Mains And Meatless Recipes

Vegetable Mains And Meatless Recipes

Baked Potato With Veggie Mix

Servings:4 | Cooking Time:45 Minutes

Ingredients:
- 4 tbsp olive oil
- 1 lb potatoes, peeled and diced
- 2 red bell peppers, halved
- 1 lb mushrooms, sliced
- 2 tomatoes, diced
- 8 garlic cloves, peeled
- 1 eggplant, sliced
- 1 yellow onion, quartered
- ½ tsp dried oregano
- ¼ tsp caraway seeds
- Salt to taste

Directions:
1. Preheat the oven to 390°F. In a bowl, combine the bell peppers, mushrooms, tomatoes, eggplant, onion, garlic, salt, olive oil, oregano, and caraway seeds. Set aside. Arrange the potatoes on a baking dish and bake for 15 minutes. Top with the veggies mixture and bake for 15-20 minutes until tender.

Nutrition Info:
- Per Serving: Calories: 302;Fat: 15g;Protein: 8.5g;-Carbs: 39g.

Roasted Artichokes

Servings:4 | Cooking Time:50 Minutes

Ingredients:
- 4 artichokes, stalk trimmed and large leaves removed
- 2 lemons, freshly squeezed
- 4 tbsp extra-virgin olive oil
- 4 cloves garlic, chopped
- 1 tsp fresh rosemary
- 1 tsp fresh basil
- 1 tsp fresh parsley
- 1 tsp fresh oregano
- Salt and black pepper to taste
- 1 tsp red pepper flakes
- 1 tsp paprika

Directions:
1. Preheat oven to 395ºF. In a small bowl, thoroughly combine the garlic with herbs and spices; set aside. Cut the artichokes in half vertically and scoop out the fibrous choke to expose the heart with a teaspoon.
2. Rub the lemon juice all over the entire surface of the artichoke halves. Arrange them on a parchment-lined baking dish, cut side up, and brush them evenly with olive oil. Stuff the cavities with the garlic/herb mixture. Cover them with aluminum foil and bake for 30 minutes. Discard the foil and bake for another 10 minutes until lightly charred. Serve.

Nutrition Info:
- Per Serving: Calories: 220;Fat: 14g;Protein: 6g;-Carbs: 21g.

Balsamic Grilled Vegetables

Servings:4 | Cooking Time:20 Minutes

Ingredients:
- ¼ cup olive oil
- 4 carrots, cut in half
- 2 onions, quartered
- 1 zucchini, cut into rounds
- 1 eggplant, cut into rounds
- 1 red bell pepper, chopped
- Salt and black pepper to taste
- Balsamic vinegar to taste

Directions:
1. Heat your grill to medium-high. Brush the vegetables lightly with olive oil, and season with salt and pepper. Grill the vegetables for 3–4 minutes per side. Transfer to a serving dish and drizzle with balsamic vinegar. Serve and enjoy!

Nutrition Info:
- Per Serving: Calories: 184;Fat: 14g;Protein: 2.1g;-Carbs: 14g.

Spinach & Lentil Stew

Servings: 4 | Cooking Time: 40 Minutes

Ingredients:

- 2 tbsp olive oil
- 1 cup dry red lentils, rinsed
- 1 carrot, chopped
- 1 celery stalk, chopped
- 1 red onion, chopped
- 4 garlic cloves, minced
- 3 tomatoes, puréed
- 3 cups vegetable broth
- 1 tsp cayenne pepper
- ½ tsp ground cumin
- ½ tsp thyme
- 1 tsp turmeric
- 1 tbsp sweet paprika
- 1 cup spinach, chopped
- 1 cup fresh cilantro, chopped
- Salt and black pepper to taste

Directions:

1. Heat the olive oil in a pot over medium heat and sauté the garlic, carrot, celery, and onion until tender, about 4-5 minutes. Stir in cayenne pepper, cumin, thyme, paprika, and turmeric for 1 minute and add tomatoes; cook for 3 more minutes. Pour in vegetable broth and lentils and bring to a boil. Reduce the heat and simmer covered for 15 minutes. Stir in spinach and cook for 5 minutes until wilted. Adjust the seasoning and divide between bowls. Top with cilantro.

Nutrition Info:

- Per Serving: Calories: 310;Fat: 9g;Protein: 18.3g;-Carbs: 41g.

Eggplant Rolls In Tomato Sauce

Servings: 4 | Cooking Time: 60 Minutes

Ingredients:

- 2 tbsp olive oil
- 1 ½ cups ricotta cheese
- 2 cans diced tomatoes
- 1 shallot, finely chopped
- 2 garlic cloves, minced
- 1 tbsp Italian seasoning
- 1 tsp dried oregano
- 2 eggplants
- ½ cup grated mozzarella
- Salt to taste
- ¼ tsp red pepper flakes

Directions:

1. Preheat oven to 350ºF. Warm olive oil in a pot over medium heat and sauté shallot and garlic for 3 minutes until tender and fragrant. Mix in tomatoes, oregano, Italian seasoning, salt, and red flakes and simmer for 6 minutes.
2. Cut the eggplants lengthwise into 1,5-inch slices and season with salt. Grill them for 2-3 minutes per side until softened. Place them on a plate and spoon 2 tbsp of ricotta cheese. Wrap them and arrange on a greased baking dish. Pour over the sauce and scatter with the mozzarella cheese. Bake for 15-20 minutes until golden-brown and bubbling.

Nutrition Info:

- Per Serving: Calories: 362;Fat: 17g;Protein: 19g;-Carbs: 38g.

Zoodles With Beet Pesto

Servings: 2 | Cooking Time: 50 Minutes

Ingredients:

- 1 medium red beet, peeled, chopped
- ½ cup walnut pieces
- ½ cup crumbled goat cheese
- 3 garlic cloves
- 2 tablespoons freshly squeezed lemon juice
- 2 tablespoons plus 2 teaspoons extra-virgin olive oil, divided
- ¼ teaspoon salt
- 4 small zucchinis, spiralized

Directions:

1. Preheat the oven to 375ºF.
2. Wrap the chopped beet in a piece of aluminum foil and seal well.
3. Roast in the preheated oven for 30 to 40 minutes until tender.
4. Meanwhile, heat a skillet over medium-high heat until hot. Add the walnuts and toast for 5 to 7 minutes, or until fragrant and lightly browned.
5. Remove the cooked beets from the oven and place in a food processor. Add the toasted walnuts, goat cheese, garlic, lemon juice, 2 tablespoons of olive oil, and salt. Pulse until smoothly blended. Set aside.
6. Heat the remaining 2 teaspoons of olive oil in a large skillet over medium heat. Add the zucchini and toss to coat in the oil. Cook for 2 to 3 minutes, stirring gently, or until the zucchini is softened.
7. Transfer the zucchini to a serving plate and toss with the beet pesto, then serve.

Nutrition Info:

- Per Serving: Calories: 423;Fat: 38.8g;Protein: 8.0g;Carbs: 17.1g.

Chickpea Lettuce Wraps With Celery

Servings: 4 | Cooking Time: 0 Minutes

Ingredients:

- 1 can low-sodium chickpeas, drained and rinsed
- 1 celery stalk, thinly sliced
- 2 tablespoons finely chopped red onion
- 2 tablespoons unsalted tahini
- 3 tablespoons honey mustard
- 1 tablespoon capers, undrained
- 12 butter lettuce leaves

Directions:

1. In a bowl, mash the chickpeas with a potato masher or the back of a fork until mostly smooth.
2. Add the celery, red onion, tahini, honey mustard, and capers to the bowl and stir until well incorporated.
3. For each serving, place three overlapping lettuce leaves on a plate and top with ¼ of the mashed chickpea filling, then roll up. Repeat with the remaining lettuce leaves and chickpea mixture.

Nutrition Info:

- Per Serving: Calories: 182;Fat: 7.1g;Protein: 10.3g;Carbs: 19.6g.

Simple Broccoli With Yogurt Sauce

Servings: 4 | Cooking Time: 25 Minutes

Ingredients:

- 2 tbsp olive oil
- 1 head broccoli, cut into florets
- 2 garlic cloves, minced
- ½ cup Greek yogurt
- Salt and black pepper to taste
- 2 tsp fresh dill, chopped

Directions:

1. Warm olive oil in a pan over medium heat and sauté broccoli, salt, and pepper for 12 minutes. Mix Greek yogurt, dill, and garlic in a small bowl. Drizzle the broccoli with the sauce.

Nutrition Info:

- Per Serving: Calories: 104;Fat: 7.7g;Protein: 4.5g;Carbs: 6g.

Homemade Vegetarian Moussaka

Servings:4 | Cooking Time:80 Minutes

Ingredients:
- 2 tbsp olive oil
- 1 yellow onion, chopped
- 2 garlic cloves, chopped
- 2 eggplants, halved
- ½ cup vegetable broth
- Salt and black pepper to taste
- ½ tsp paprika
- ¼ cup parsley, chopped
- 1 tsp basil, chopped
- 1 tsp hot sauce
- 1 tomato, chopped
- 2 tbsp tomato puree
- 6 Kalamata olives, chopped
- ½ cup feta cheese, crumbled

Directions:

1. Preheat oven to 360ºF. Remove the tender center part of the eggplants and chop it. Arrange the eggplant halves on a baking tray and drizzle with some olive oil. Roast for 35-40 minutes.
2. Warm the remaining olive oil in a skillet over medium heat and add eggplant flesh, onion, and garlic and sauté for 5 minutes until tender. Stir in the vegetable broth, salt, pepper, basil, hot sauce, paprika, tomato, and tomato puree. Lower the heat and simmer for 10-15 minutes. Once the eggplants are ready, remove them from the oven and fill them with the mixture. Top with Kalamata olives and feta cheese. Return to the oven and bake for 10-15 minutes. Sprinkle with parsley.

Nutrition Info:
- Per Serving: Calories: 223;Fat: 14g;Protein: 6.9g;-Carbs: 23g.

Spicy Kale With Almonds

Servings:4 | Cooking Time:25 Minutes

Ingredients:
- 2 tbsp olive oil
- ¼ cup slivered almonds
- 1 lb chopped kale
- ¼ cup vegetable broth
- 1 lemon, juiced and zested
- 1 garlic clove, minced
- 1 tbsp red pepper flakes
- Salt and black pepper to taste

Directions:

1. Warm olive oil in a pan over medium heat and sauté garlic, kale, salt, and pepper for 8-9 minutes until soft. Add in lemon juice, lemon zest, red pepper flakes, and vegetable broth and continue cooking until the liquid evaporates, about 3-5 minutes. Garnish with almonds and serve.

Nutrition Info:
- Per Serving: Calories: 123;Fat: 8.1g;Protein: 4g;-Carbs: 10.8g.

Tradicional Matchuba Green Beans

Servings:4 | Cooking Time:15 Minutes

Ingredients:
- 1 ¼ lb narrow green beans, trimmed
- 3 tbsp butter, melted
- 1 cup Moroccan matbucha
- 2 green onions, chopped
- Salt and black pepper to taste

Directions:

1. Steam the green beans in a pot for 5-6 minutes until tender. Remove to a bowl, reserving the cooking liquid. In a skillet over medium heat, melt the butter. Add in green onions, salt, and black pepper and cook until fragrant. Lower the heat and put in the green beans along with some of the reserved water. Simmer for 3-4 minutes. Serve the green beans with the Sabra Moroccan matbucha as a dip.

Nutrition Info:
- Per Serving: Calories: 125;Fat: 8.6g;Protein: 2.2g;-Carbs: 9g.

Creamy Polenta With Mushrooms

Servings: 2 | Cooking Time: 30 Minutes

Ingredients:
- ½ ounce dried porcini mushrooms (optional but recommended)
- 2 tablespoons olive oil
- 1 pound baby bella (cremini) mushrooms, quartered
- 1 large shallot, minced
- 1 garlic clove, minced
- 1 tablespoon flour
- 2 teaspoons tomato paste
- ½ cup red wine
- 1 cup mushroom stock (or reserved liquid from soaking the porcini mushrooms, if using)
- ½ teaspoon dried thyme
- 1 fresh rosemary sprig
- 1½ cups water
- ½ teaspoon salt
- ⅓ cup instant polenta
- 2 tablespoons grated Parmesan cheese

Directions:

1. If using the dried porcini mushrooms, soak them in 1 cup of hot water for about 15 minutes to soften them. When they're softened, scoop them out of the water, reserving the soaking liquid. Mince the porcini mushrooms.
2. Heat the olive oil in a large sauté pan over medium-high heat. Add the mushrooms, shallot, and garlic, and sauté for 10 minutes, or until the vegetables are wilted and starting to caramelize.
3. Add the flour and tomato paste, and cook for another 30 seconds. Add the red wine, mushroom stock or porcini soaking liquid, thyme, and rosemary. Bring the mixture to a boil, stirring constantly until it thickens. Reduce the heat and let it simmer for 10 minutes.
4. Meanwhile, bring the water to a boil in a saucepan and add salt.
5. Add the instant polenta and stir quickly while it thickens. Stir in the Parmesan cheese. Taste and add additional salt, if needed. Serve warm.

Nutrition Info:
- Per Serving: Calories: 450;Fat: 16.0g;Protein: 14.1g;Carbs: 57.8g.

Parsley & Olive Zucchini Bake

Servings: 6 | Cooking Time: 1 Hour 40 Minutes

Ingredients:
- 3 tbsp olive oil
- 1 can tomatoes, diced
- 2 lb zucchinis, sliced
- 1 onion, chopped
- Salt and black pepper to taste
- 3 garlic cloves, minced
- ¼ tsp dried oregano
- ¼ tsp red pepper flakes
- 10 Kalamata olives, chopped
- 2 tbsp fresh parsley, chopped

Directions:

1. Preheat oven to 325ºF. Warm the olive oil in a saucepan over medium heat. Sauté zucchini for about 3 minutes per side; transfer to a bowl. Stir-fry the onion and salt in the same saucepan for 3-5 minutes, stirring occasionally until onion soft and lightly golden. Stir in garlic, oregano, and pepper flakes and cook until fragrant, about 30 seconds.
2. Add in olives, tomatoes, salt, and pepper, bring to a simmer, and cook for about 10 minutes, stirring occasionally. Return the zucchini, cover, and transfer the pot to the oven. Bake for 10-15 minutes. Sprinkle with parsley and serve.

Nutrition Info:
- Per Serving: Calories: 164;Fat: 6g;Protein: 1.5g;Carbs: 7.7g.

Baked Vegetable Stew

Servings:6 | Cooking Time:70 Minutes

Ingredients:

- 1 can diced tomatoes, drained with juice reserved
- 3 tbsp olive oil
- 1 onion, chopped
- 2 tbsp fresh oregano, minced
- 1 tsp paprika
- 4 garlic cloves, minced
- 1 ½ lb green beans, sliced
- 1 lb Yukon Gold potatoes, peeled and chopped
- 1 tbsp tomato paste
- Salt and black pepper to taste
- 3 tbsp fresh basil, chopped

Directions:

1. Preheat oven to 360°F. Warm the olive oil in a skillet over medium heat. Sauté onion and garlic for 3 minutes until softened. Stir in oregano and paprika for 30 seconds. Transfer to a baking dish and add in green beans, potatoes, tomatoes, tomato paste, salt, pepper, and 1 ½ cups of water; stir well. Bake for 40-50 minutes. Sprinkle with basil. Serve.

Nutrition Info:

- Per Serving: Calories: 121;Fat: 0.8g;Protein: 4.2g;Carbs: 26g.

Baked Honey Acorn Squash

Servings:4 | Cooking Time:35 Minutes

Ingredients:

- 1 acorn squash, cut into wedges
- 2 tbsp olive oil
- 2 tbsp honey
- 2 tbsp rosemary, chopped
- 2 tbsp walnuts, chopped

Directions:

1. Preheat oven to 400°F. In a bowl, mix honey, rosemary, and olive oil. Lay the squash wedges on a baking sheet and drizzle with the honey mixture. Bake for 30 minutes until squash is tender and slightly caramelized, turning each slice over halfway through. Serve cooled sprinkled with walnuts.

Nutrition Info:

- Per Serving: Calories: 136;Fat: 6g;Protein: 0.9g;Carbs: 20g.

Grilled Eggplant "steaks" With Sauce

Servings:6 | Cooking Time:20 Minutes

Ingredients:

- 2 lb eggplants, sliced lengthways
- 6 tbsp olive oil
- 5 garlic cloves, minced
- 1 tsp dried oregano
- ½ tsp red pepper flakes
- ½ cup Greek yogurt
- 3 tbsp chopped fresh parsley
- 1 tsp grated lemon zest
- 2 tsp lemon juice
- 1 tsp ground cumin
- Salt and black pepper to taste

Directions:

1. In a bowl, whisk half of the olive oil, yogurt, parsley, lemon zest and juice, cumin, and salt; set aside until ready to serve. Preheat your grill to High. Rub the eggplant steaks with the remaining olive oil, oregano, salt, and pepper. Grill them for 4-6 minutes per side until browned and tender; transfer to a serving platter. Drizzle yogurt sauce over eggplant.

Nutrition Info:

- Per Serving: Calories: 112;Fat: 7g;Protein: 2.6g;Carbs: 11.3g.

Cauliflower Cakes With Goat Cheese

Servings: 4 | Cooking Time: 50 Minutes

Ingredients:
- ¼ cup olive oil
- 10 oz cauliflower florets
- 1 tsp ground turmeric
- 1 tsp ground coriander
- Salt and black pepper to taste
- ½ tsp ground mustard seeds
- 4 oz Goat cheese, softened
- 2 scallions, sliced thin
- 1 large egg, lightly beaten
- 2 garlic cloves, minced
- 1 tsp grated lemon zest
- 4 lemon wedges
- ¼ cup flour

Directions:

1. Preheat oven to 420°F. In a bowl, whisk 1 tablespoon oil, turmeric, coriander, salt, ground mustard, and pepper. Add in the cauliflower and toss to coat. Transfer to a greased baking sheet and spread it in a single layer. Roast for 20-25 minutes until cauliflower is well browned and tender. Transfer the cauliflower to a large bowl and mash it coarsely with a potato masher. Stir in Goat cheese, scallions, egg, garlic, and lemon zest until well combined. Sprinkle flour over cauliflower mixture and stir to incorporate. Shape the mixture into 10-12 cakes and place them on a sheet pan. Chill to firm, about 30 minutes. Warm the remaining olive oil in a skillet over medium heat. Fry the cakes for 5-6 minutes on each side until deep golden brown and crisp. Serve with lemon wedges.

Nutrition Info:
- Per Serving: Calories: 320;Fat: 25g;Protein: 13g;-Carbs: 12g.

Veggie-stuffed Portabello Mushrooms

Servings: 6 | Cooking Time: 24 To 25 Minutes

Ingredients:
- 3 tablespoons extra-virgin olive oil, divided
- 1 cup diced onion
- 2 garlic cloves, minced
- 1 large zucchini, diced
- 3 cups chopped mushrooms
- 1 cup chopped tomato
- 1 teaspoon dried oregano
- ¼ teaspoon kosher salt
- ¼ teaspoon crushed red pepper
- 6 large portabello mushrooms, stems and gills removed
- Cooking spray
- 4 ounces fresh Mozzarella cheese, shredded

Directions:

1. In a large skillet over medium heat, heat 2 tablespoons of the oil. Add the onion and sauté for 4 minutes. Stir in the garlic and sauté for 1 minute.
2. Stir in the zucchini, mushrooms, tomato, oregano, salt and red pepper. Cook for 10 minutes, stirring constantly. Remove from the heat.
3. Meanwhile, heat a grill pan over medium-high heat.
4. Brush the remaining 1 tablespoon of the oil over the portabello mushroom caps. Place the mushrooms, bottom-side down, on the grill pan. Cover with a sheet of aluminum foil sprayed with nonstick cooking spray. Cook for 5 minutes.
5. Flip the mushroom caps over, and spoon about ½ cup of the cooked vegetable mixture into each cap. Top each with about 2½ tablespoons of the Mozzarella.
6. Cover and grill for 4 to 5 minutes, or until the cheese is melted.
7. Using a spatula, transfer the portabello mushrooms to a plate. Let cool for about 5 minutes before serving.

Nutrition Info:
- Per Serving: Calories: 111;Fat: 4.0g;Protein: 11.0g;-Carbs: 11.0g.

Mini Crustless Spinach Quiches

Servings: 6 | Cooking Time: 20 Minutes

Ingredients:

- 2 tablespoons extra-virgin olive oil
- 1 onion, finely chopped
- 2 cups baby spinach
- 2 garlic cloves, minced
- 8 large eggs, beaten
- ¼ cup unsweetened almond milk
- ½ teaspoon sea salt
- ¼ teaspoon freshly ground black pepper
- 1 cup shredded Swiss cheese
- Cooking spray

Directions:

1. Preheat the oven to 375°F. Spritz a 6-cup muffin tin with cooking spray. Set aside.
2. In a large skillet over medium-high heat, heat the olive oil until shimmering. Add the onion and cook for about 4 minutes, or until soft. Add the spinach and cook for about 1 minute, stirring constantly, or until the spinach softens. Add the garlic and sauté for 30 seconds. Remove from the heat and let cool.
3. In a medium bowl, whisk together the eggs, milk, salt and pepper.
4. Stir the cooled vegetables and the cheese into the egg mixture. Spoon the mixture into the prepared muffin tins. Bake for about 15 minutes, or until the eggs are set.
5. Let rest for 5 minutes before serving.

Nutrition Info:

- Per Serving: Calories: 218;Fat: 17.0g;Protein: 14.0g;Carbs: 4.0g.

Zucchini Crisp

Servings: 2 | Cooking Time: 20 Minutes

Ingredients:

- 4 zucchinis, sliced into ½-inch rounds
- ½ cup unsweetened almond milk
- 1 teaspoon fresh lemon juice
- 1 teaspoon arrowroot powder
- ½ teaspoon salt, divided
- ½ cup whole wheat bread crumbs
- ¼ cup nutritional yeast
- ¼ cup hemp seeds
- ½ teaspoon garlic powder
- ¼ teaspoon crushed red pepper
- ¼ teaspoon black pepper

Directions:

1. Preheat the oven to 375°F. Line two baking sheets with parchment paper and set aside.
2. Put the zucchini in a medium bowl with the almond milk, lemon juice, arrowroot powder, and ¼ teaspoon of salt. Stir to mix well.
3. In a large bowl with a lid, thoroughly combine the bread crumbs, nutritional yeast, hemp seeds, garlic powder, crushed red pepper and black pepper. Add the zucchini in batches and shake until the slices are evenly coated.
4. Arrange the zucchini on the prepared baking sheets in a single layer.
5. Bake in the preheated oven for about 20 minutes, or until the zucchini slices are golden brown.
6. Season with the remaining ¼ teaspoon of salt before serving.

Nutrition Info:

- Per Serving: Calories: 255;Fat: 11.3g;Protein: 8.6g;Carbs: 31.9g.

Spicy Roasted Tomatoes

Servings: 2 | Cooking Time: 50 Minutes

Ingredients:
- ¼ cup olive oil
- 1 lb mixed cherry tomatoes
- 10 garlic cloves, minced
- Salt to taste
- 1 fresh rosemary sprig
- 1 fresh thyme sprig
- 2 crusty bread slices

Directions:
1. Preheat oven to 350ºF. Toss the cherry tomatoes, garlic, olive oil, and salt in a baking dish. Top with the herb sprigs. Roast the tomatoes for about 45 minutes until they are soft and begin to caramelize. Discard the herbs and serve with bread.

Nutrition Info:
- Per Serving: Calories: 271;Fat: 26g;Protein: 3g;-Carbs: 12g.

Minty Broccoli & Walnuts

Servings: 2 | Cooking Time: 10 Minutes

Ingredients:
- 1 garlic clove, minced
- ½ cups walnuts, chopped
- 3 cups broccoli florets, steamed
- 1 tbsp mint, chopped
- ½ lemon, juiced
- Salt and black pepper to taste

Directions:
1. Mix walnuts, broccoli, garlic, mint, lemon juice, salt, and pepper in a bowl. Serve chilled.

Nutrition Info:
- Per Serving: Calories: 210;Fat: 7g;Protein: 4g;Carbs: 9g.

Moroccan Tagine With Vegetables

Servings: 2 | Cooking Time: 40 Minutes

Ingredients:
- 2 tablespoons olive oil
- ½ onion, diced
- 1 garlic clove, minced
- 2 cups cauliflower florets
- 1 medium carrot, cut into 1-inch pieces
- 1 cup diced eggplant
- 1 can whole tomatoes with their juices
- 1 can chickpeas, drained and rinsed
- 2 small red potatoes, cut into 1-inch pieces
- 1 cup water
- 1 teaspoon pure maple syrup
- ½ teaspoon cinnamon
- ½ teaspoon turmeric
- 1 teaspoon cumin
- ½ teaspoon salt
- 1 to 2 teaspoons harissa paste

Directions:
1. In a Dutch oven, heat the olive oil over medium-high heat. Sauté the onion for 5 minutes, stirring occasionally, or until the onion is translucent.
2. Stir in the garlic, cauliflower florets, carrot, eggplant, tomatoes, and potatoes. Using a wooden spoon or spatula to break up the tomatoes into smaller pieces.
3. Add the chickpeas, water, maple syrup, cinnamon, turmeric, cumin, and salt and stir to incorporate. Bring the mixture to a boil.
4. Once it starts to boil, reduce the heat to medium-low. Stir in the harissa paste, cover, allow to simmer for about 40 minutes, or until the vegetables are softened. Taste and adjust seasoning as needed.
5. Let the mixture cool for 5 minutes before serving.

Nutrition Info:
- Per Serving: Calories: 293;Fat: 9.9g;Protein: 11.2g;-Carbs: 45.5g.

Sweet Mustard Cabbage Hash

Servings: 4 | Cooking Time: 30 Minutes

Ingredients:
- 1 head Savoy cabbage, shredded
- 3 tbsp olive oil
- 1 onion, finely chopped
- 2 garlic cloves, minced
- ½ tsp fennel seeds
- ¼ cup red wine vinegar
- 1 tbsp mustard powder
- 1 tbsp honey
- Salt and black pepper to taste

Directions:

1. Warm olive oil in a pan over medium heat and sauté onion, fennel seeds, cabbage, salt, and pepper for 8-9 minutes.
2. In a bowl, mix vinegar, mustard, and honey; set aside. Sauté garlic in the pan for 30 seconds. Pour in vinegar mixture and cook for 10-15 minutes until the liquid reduces by half.

Nutrition Info:
- Per Serving: Calories: 181;Fat: 12g;Protein: 3.4g;-Carbs: 19g.

Rainbow Vegetable Kebabs

Servings: 4 | Cooking Time: 30 Minutes

Ingredients:
- 1 cup mushrooms, cut into quarters
- 6 mixed bell peppers, cut into squares
- 4 red onions, cut into 6 wedges
- 4 zucchini, cut into half-moons
- 2 tomatoes, cut into quarters
- 3 tbsp herbed oil

Directions:

1. Preheat your grill to medium-high. Alternate the vegetables onto bamboo skewers. Grill them for 5 minutes on each side until the vegetables begin to char. Remove them from heat and drizzle with herbed oil.

Nutrition Info:
- Per Serving: Calories: 238;Fat: 12g;Protein: 6g;-Carbs: 34.2g.

Parmesan Stuffed Zucchini Boats

Servings: 4 | Cooking Time: 15 Minutes

Ingredients:
- 1 cup canned low-sodium chickpeas, drained and rinsed
- 1 cup no-sugar-added spaghetti sauce
- 2 zucchinis
- ¼ cup shredded Parmesan cheese

Directions:

1. Preheat the oven to 425°F.
2. In a medium bowl, stir together the chickpeas and spaghetti sauce.
3. Cut the zucchini in half lengthwise and scrape a spoon gently down the length of each half to remove the seeds.
4. Fill each zucchini half with the chickpea sauce and top with one-quarter of the Parmesan cheese.
5. Place the zucchini halves on a baking sheet and roast in the oven for 15 minutes.
6. Transfer to a plate. Let rest for 5 minutes before serving.

Nutrition Info:
- Per Serving: Calories: 139;Fat: 4.0g;Protein: 8.0g;-Carbs: 20.0g.

Simple Honey-glazed Baby Carrots

Servings:2 | Cooking Time: 6 Minutes

Ingredients:

- ⅔ cup water
- 1½ pounds baby carrots
- 4 tablespoons almond butter
- ½ cup honey
- 1 teaspoon dried thyme
- 1½ teaspoons dried dill
- Salt, to taste

Directions:

1. Pour the water into the Instant Pot and add a steamer basket. Place the baby carrots in the basket.
2. Secure the lid. Select the Manual mode and set the cooking time for 4 minutes at High Pressure.
3. Once cooking is complete, do a quick pressure release. Carefully open the lid.
4. Transfer the carrots to a plate and set aside.
5. Pour the water out of the Instant Pot and dry it.
6. Press the Sauté button on the Instant Pot and heat the almond butter.
7. Stir in the honey, thyme, and dill.
8. Return the carrots to the Instant Pot and stir until well coated. Sauté for another 1 minute.
9. Taste and season with salt as needed. Serve warm.

Nutrition Info:

- Per Serving: Calories: 575;Fat: 23.5g;Protein: 2.8g;-Carbs: 90.6g.

Tasty Lentil Burgers

Servings:4 | Cooking Time:25 Minutes

Ingredients:

- 1 cup cremini mushrooms, finely chopped
- 1 cup cooked green lentils
- ½ cup Greek yogurt
- ½ lemon, zested and juiced
- ½ tsp garlic powder
- ½ tsp dried oregano
- 1 tbsp fresh cilantro, chopped
- Salt to taste
- 3 tbsp extra-virgin olive oil
- ¼ tsp tbsp white miso
- ¼ tsp smoked paprika
- ¼ cup flour

Directions:

1. Pour ½ cup of lentils in your blender and puree partially until somewhat smooth, but with many whole lentils still remaining. In a small bowl, mix the yogurt, lemon zest and juice, garlic powder, oregano, cilantro, and salt. Season and set aside. In a medium bowl, mix the mushrooms, 2 tablespoons of olive oil, miso, and paprika. Stir in all the lentils. Add in flour and stir until the mixture everything is well incorporated. Shape the mixture into patties about ¾-inch thick. Warm the remaining olive oil in a skillet over medium heat. Fry the patties until browned and crisp, about 3 minutes. Turn and fry on the second side. Serve with the reserved yogurt mixture.

Nutrition Info:

- Per Serving: Calories: 215;Fat: 13g;Protein: 10g;-Carbs: 19g.

Fish And Seafood Recipes

Fish And Seafood Recipes

Parsley Littleneck Clams In Sherry Sauce

Servings:4 | Cooking Time:20 Minutes

Ingredients:
- 2 tbsp olive oil
- 1 cup dry sherry
- 3 shallots, minced
- 4 garlic cloves, minced
- 4 lb littleneck clams, scrubbed
- 2 tbsp minced fresh parsley
- ½ tsp cayenne pepper
- 1 Lemon, cut into wedges

Directions:
1. Bring the sherry wine, shallots, and garlic to a simmer in a large saucepan and cook for 3 minutes. Add clams, cover, and cook, stirring twice, until clams open, about 7 minutes. With a slotted spoon, transfer clams to a serving bowl, discarding any that refuse to open. Stir in olive oil, parsley, and cayenne pepper. Pour sauce over clams and serve with lemon wedges.

Nutrition Info:
- Per Serving: Calories: 333;Fat: 9g;Protein: 44.9g;Carbs: 14g.

Baked Oysters With Vegetables

Servings:2 | Cooking Time: 15 To 17 Minutes

Ingredients:
- 2 cups coarse salt, for holding the oysters
- 1 dozen fresh oysters, scrubbed
- 1 tablespoon almond butter
- ¼ cup finely chopped scallions, both white and green parts
- ½ cup finely chopped artichoke hearts
- ¼ cup finely chopped red bell pepper
- 1 garlic clove, minced
- 1 tablespoon finely chopped fresh parsley
- Zest and juice of ½ lemon
- Pinch salt
- Freshly ground black pepper, to taste

Directions:
1. Pour the salt into a baking dish and spread to evenly fill the bottom of the dish.
2. Prepare a clean work surface to shuck the oysters. Using a shucking knife, insert the blade at the joint of the shell, where it hinges open and shut. Firmly apply pressure to pop the blade in, and work the knife around the shell to open. Discard the empty half of the shell. Using the knife, gently loosen the oyster, and remove any shell particles. Set the oysters in their shells on the salt, being careful not to spill the juices.
3. Preheat the oven to 425°F.
4. Heat the almond butter in a large skillet over medium heat. Add the scallions, artichoke hearts, and bell pepper, and cook for 5 to 7 minutes. Add the garlic and cook for 1 minute more.
5. Remove from the heat and stir in the parsley, lemon zest and juice, and season to taste with salt and pepper.
6. Divide the vegetable mixture evenly among the oysters. Bake in the preheated oven for 10 to 12 minutes, or until the vegetables are lightly browned. Serve warm.

Nutrition Info:
- Per Serving: Calories: 135;Fat: 7.2g;Protein: 6.0g;Carbs: 10.7g.

Roasted Red Snapper With Citrus Topping

Servings:2 | Cooking Time:35 Minutes

Ingredients:

- 2 tbsp olive oil
- 1 tsp fresh cilantro, chopped
- ½ tsp grated lemon zest
- ½ tbsp lemon juice
- ½ tsp grated grapefruit zest
- ½ tbsp grapefruit juice
- ½ tsp grated orange zest
- ½ tbsp orange juice
- ½ shallot, minced
- ¼ tsp red pepper flakes
- Salt and black pepper to taste
- 1 whole red snapper, cleaned

Directions:

1. Preheat oven to 380°F. Whisk the olive oil, cilantro, lemon juice, orange juice, grapefruit juice, shallot, and pepper flakes together in a bowl. Season with salt and pepper. Set aside the citrus topping until ready to serve.
2. In a separate bowl, combine lemon zest, orange zest, grapefruit zest, salt, and pepper. With a sharp knife, make 3-4 shallow slashes, about 2 inches apart, on both sides of the snapper. Spoon the citrus mixture into the fish cavity and transfer to a greased baking sheet. Roast for 25 minutes until the fish flakes. Serve drizzled with citrus topping, and enjoy!

Nutrition Info:

- Per Serving: Calories: 257;Fat: 21g;Protein: 16g;-Carbs: 1.6g.

Spicy Cod Fillets

Servings:4 | Cooking Time:35 Minutes

Ingredients:

- 2 tbsp olive oil
- 1 tsp lime juice
- Salt and black pepper to taste
- 1 tsp sweet paprika
- 1 tsp chili powder
- 1 onion, chopped
- 2 garlic cloves, minced
- 4 cod fillets, boneless
- 1 tsp ground coriander
- ½ cup fish stock
- ½ lb cherry tomatoes, cubed

Directions:

1. Warm olive oil in a skillet over medium heat. Season the cod with salt, pepper, and chili powder and cook in the skillet for 8 minutes on all sides; set aside. In the same skillet, cook onion and garlic for 3 minutes. Stir in lime juice, paprika, coriander, fish stock, and cherry tomatoes and bring to a boil. Simmer for 10 minutes. Serve topped with cod fillets.

Nutrition Info:

- Per Serving: Calories: 240;Fat: 17g;Protein: 17g;-Carbs: 26g.

Baked Anchovies With Chili-garlic Topping

Servings:2 | Cooking Time:10 Minutes

Ingredients:

- ½ tsp red pepper flakes
- 16 canned anchovies
- 4 garlic cloves, minced
- Salt and black pepper to taste

Directions:

1. Preheat the broiler. Arrange the anchovies on a foil-lined baking dish. In a bowl, mix anchovy olive oil, garlic, salt, red flakes, and pepper and pour over anchovies. Broil for 3-4 minutes. Divide between 4 plates and drizzle with the remaining mixture from the dish. Serve and enjoy!

Nutrition Info:

- Per Serving: Calories: 103;Fat: 3g;Protein: 11g;-Carbs: 5g.

Shrimp & Salmon In Tomato Sauce

Servings: 4 | Cooking Time: 30 Minutes

Ingredients:

- 1 lb shrimp, peeled and deveined
- 2 tbsp olive oil
- 1 lb salmon fillets
- Salt and black pepper to taste
- 1 cups tomatoes, chopped
- 1 onion, chopped
- 2 garlic cloves, minced
- ¼ tsp red pepper flakes
- 1 cup fish stock
- 1 tbsp cilantro, chopped

Directions:

1. Preheat the oven to 360°F. Line a baking sheet with parchment paper. Season the salmon with salt and pepper, drizzle with some olive oil, and arrange them on the sheet. Bake for 15 minutes. Remove to a serving plate.
2. Warm the remaining olive oil in a skillet over medium heat and sauté onion and garlic for 3 minutes until tender. Pour in tomatoes, fish stock, salt, pepper, and red pepper flakes and bring to a boil. Simmer for 10 minutes. Stir in shrimp and cook for another 8 minutes. Pour the sauce over the salmon and serve sprinkled with cilantro.

Nutrition Info:

- Per Serving: Calories: 240;Fat: 16g;Protein: 18g;-Carbs: 22g.

Lemony Shrimp With Orzo Salad

Servings: 4 | Cooking Time: 22 Minutes

Ingredients:

- 1 cup orzo
- 1 hothouse cucumber, deseeded and chopped
- ½ cup finely diced red onion
- 2 tablespoons extra-virgin olive oil
- 2 pounds shrimp, peeled and deveined
- 3 lemons, juiced
- Salt and freshly ground black pepper, to taste
- ¾ cup crumbled feta cheese
- 2 tablespoons dried dill
- 1 cup chopped fresh flat-leaf parsley

Directions:

1. Bring a large pot of water to a boil. Add the orzo and cook covered for 15 to 18 minutes, or until the orzo is tender. Transfer to a colander to drain and set aside to cool.
2. Mix the cucumber and red onion in a bowl. Set aside.
3. Heat the olive oil in a medium skillet over medium heat until it shimmers.
4. Reduce the heat, add the shrimp, and cook each side for 2 minutes until cooked through.
5. Add the cooked shrimp to the bowl of cucumber and red onion. Mix in the cooked orzo and lemon juice and toss to combine. Sprinkle with salt and pepper. Scatter the top with the feta cheese and dill. Garnish with the parsley and serve immediately.

Nutrition Info:

- Per Serving: Calories: 565;Fat: 17.8g;Protein: 63.3g;Carbs: 43.9g.

Fennel & Bell Pepper Salmon

Servings:4 | Cooking Time:30 Minutes

Ingredients:

- 2 tbsp olive oil
- 4 salmon fillets, boneless
- 1 fennel bulb, sliced
- Salt and black pepper to taste
- ½ tsp chili powder
- 1 yellow bell pepper, diced
- 1 red bell pepper, chopped
- 1 green bell pepper, chopped

Directions:

1. Warm olive oil in a skillet over medium heat. Season the salmon with chili powder, salt, and pepper and cook for 6-8 minutes, turning once. Remove to a serving plate. Add fennel and peppers to the skillet and cook for another 10 minutes until tender. Top the salmon with the mixture.

Nutrition Info:

- Per Serving: Calories: 580;Fat: 19g;Protein: 35g;-Carbs: 73g.

Mustard Sardine Cakes

Servings:4 | Cooking Time:20 Minutes

Ingredients:

- 3 tbsp olive oil
- 1 tsp mustard powder
- 1 tsp chili powder
- 20 oz canned sardines, mashed
- 2 garlic cloves, minced
- 2 tbsp dill, chopped
- 1 onion, chopped
- 1 cup panko breadcrumbs
- 1 egg, whisked
- Salt and black pepper to taste
- 2 tbsp lemon juice

Directions:

1. Combine sardines, garlic, dill, onion, breadcrumbs, egg, mustard powder, chili powder, salt, pepper, and lemon juice in a bowl and form medium patties out of the mixture. Warm the olive oil in a skillet over medium heat and fry the cakes for 10 minutes on both sides. Serve with aioli.

Nutrition Info:

- Per Serving: Calories: 300;Fat: 14g;Protein: 7g;-Carbs: 23g.

Salmon Stuffed Peppers

Servings:4 | Cooking Time:25 Minutes

Ingredients:

- 4 bell peppers
- 10 oz canned salmon, drained
- 12 black olives, chopped
- 1 red onion, finely chopped
- ½ tsp garlic, minced
- 1/3 cup mayonnaise
- 1 cup cream cheese
- 1 tsp Mediterranean seasoning
- Salt and pepper flakes to taste

Directions:

1. Preheat oven to 390 °F. Cut the peppers into halves and remove the seeds. In a mixing bowl, combine the salmon, onion, garlic, mayonnaise, olives, salt, red pepper, Mediterranean spice mix, and cream cheese. Divide the mixture between the peppers and bake them in the oven for 10-12 minutes or until cooked through. Serve and enjoy!

Nutrition Info:

- Per Serving: Calories: 272;Fat: 14g;Protein: 29g;-Carbs: 5g.

Anchovy Spread With Avocado

Servings:2 | Cooking Time:5 Minutes

Ingredients:

- 1 avocado, peeled and pitted
- 1 tsp lemon juice
- ¼ celery stalk, chopped
- ¼ cup chopped shallots
- 2 anchovy fillets in olive oil
- Salt and black pepper to taste

Directions:

1. Combine lemon juice, avocado, celery, shallots, and anchovy fillets (with their olive oil) in a food processor. Blitz until smooth. Season with salt and black pepper. Serve.

Nutrition Info:

- Per Serving: Calories: 271;Fat: 20g;Protein: 15g;-Carbs: 12g.

Salmon And Mushroom Hash With Pesto

Servings: 6 | Cooking Time: 20 Minutes

Ingredients:

- Pesto:
- ¼ cup extra-virgin olive oil
- 1 bunch fresh basil
- Juice and zest of 1 lemon
- ⅓ cup water
- ¼ teaspoon salt, plus additional as needed
- Hash:
- 2 tablespoons extra-virgin olive oil
- 6 cups mixed mushrooms (brown, white, shiitake, cremini, portobello, etc.), sliced
- 1 pound wild salmon, cubed

Directions:

1. Make the pesto: Pulse the olive oil, basil, juice and zest, water, and salt in a blender or food processor until smoothly blended. Set aside.
2. Heat the olive oil in a large skillet over medium heat.
3. Stir-fry the mushrooms for 6 to 8 minutes, or until they begin to exude their juices.
4. Add the salmon and cook each side for 5 to 6 minutes until cooked through.
5. Fold in the prepared pesto and stir well. Taste and add additional salt as needed. Serve warm.

Nutrition Info:

- Per Serving: Calories: 264;Fat: 14.7g;Protein: 7.0g;-Carbs: 30.9g.

Baked Cod With Lemony Rice

Servings: 4 | Cooking Time: 45 Minutes

Ingredients:

- 2 tbsp olive oil
- 1 cup rice
- 1 garlic clove, minced
- 1 tsp red pepper, crushed
- 2 shallots, chopped
- 1 tsp anchovy paste
- 1 tbsp oregano, chopped
- 6 black olives, chopped
- 2 tbsp capers, drained
- 1 tsp paprika
- 15 oz canned tomatoes, diced
- Salt and black pepper to taste
- 4 cod fillets, boneless
- 1 oz feta cheese, crumbled
- 1 tbsp parsley, chopped
- 2 cups chicken stock
- 1 lemon, zested

Directions:

1. Preheat the oven to 360ºF. Warm the olive oil in a skillet over medium heat. Sauté the garlic, red pepper, and shallot for 5 minutes. Stir in anchovy paste, paprika, oregano, olives, capers, tomatoes, salt, and pepper and cook for another 5 minutes. Put in cod fillets and top with the feta cheese and parsley. Bake for 15 minutes.
2. In the meantime, boil chicken stock in a pot over medium heat. Add in rice and lemon zest, bring to a simmer, and cook for 15-18 minutes. When ready, fluff with a fork. Share the rice into plates and top with cod mixture. Serve warm.

Nutrition Info:

- Per Serving: Calories: 410;Fat: 22g;Protein: 32g;-Carbs: 22g.

Spicy Haddock Stew

Servings: 6 | Cooking Time: 35 Minutes

Ingredients:

- ¼ cup coconut oil
- 1 tablespoon minced garlic
- 1 onion, chopped
- 2 celery stalks, chopped
- ½ fennel bulb, thinly sliced
- 1 carrot, diced
- 1 sweet potato, diced
- 1 can low-sodium diced tomatoes
- 1 cup coconut milk
- 1 cup low-sodium chicken broth
- ¼ teaspoon red pepper flakes
- 12 ounces haddock, cut into 1-inch chunks
- 2 tablespoons chopped fresh cilantro, for garnish

Directions:

1. In a large saucepan, heat the coconut oil over medium-high heat.
2. Add the garlic, onion, and celery and sauté for about 4 minutes, stirring occasionally, or until they are tender.
3. Stir in the fennel bulb, carrot, and sweet potato and sauté for 4 minutes more.
4. Add the diced tomatoes, coconut milk, chicken broth, and red pepper flakes and stir to incorporate, then bring the mixture to a boil.
5. Once it starts to boil, reduce the heat to low, and bring to a simmer for about 15 minutes, or until the vegetables are fork-tender.
6. Add the haddock chunks and continue simmering for about 10 minutes, or until the fish is cooked through.
7. Sprinkle the cilantro on top for garnish before serving.

Nutrition Info:

- Per Serving: Calories: 276;Fat: 20.9g;Protein: 14.2g;Carbs: 6.8g.

Shrimp And Pea Paella

Servings: 2 | Cooking Time: 60 Minutes

Ingredients:

- 2 tablespoons olive oil
- 1 garlic clove, minced
- ½ large onion, minced
- 1 cup diced tomato
- ½ cup short-grain rice
- ½ teaspoon sweet paprika
- ½ cup dry white wine
- 1¼ cups low-sodium chicken stock
- 8 ounces large raw shrimp
- 1 cup frozen peas
- ¼ cup jarred roasted red peppers, cut into strips
- Salt, to taste

Directions:

1. Heat the olive oil in a large skillet over medium-high heat.
2. Add the garlic and onion and sauté for 3 minutes, or until the onion is softened.
3. Add the tomato, rice, and paprika and stir for 3 minutes to toast the rice.
4. Add the wine and chicken stock and stir to combine. Bring the mixture to a boil.
5. Cover and reduce the heat to medium-low, and simmer for 45 minutes, or until the rice is just about tender and most of the liquid has been absorbed.
6. Add the shrimp, peas, and roasted red peppers. Cover and cook for an additional 5 minutes. Season with salt to taste and serve.

Nutrition Info:

- Per Serving: Calories: 646;Fat: 27.1g;Protein: 42.0g;Carbs: 59.7g.

Walnut-crusted Salmon

Servings: 4 | Cooking Time: 25 Minutes

Ingredients:

- 2 tbsp olive oil
- 4 salmon fillets, boneless
- 2 tbsp mustard
- 5 tsp honey
- 1 cup walnuts, chopped
- 1 tbsp lemon juice
- 2 tsp parsley, chopped
- Salt and pepper to the taste

Directions:

1. Preheat the oven to 380°F. Line a baking tray with parchment paper. In a bowl, whisk the olive oil, mustard, and honey. In a separate bowl, combine walnuts and parsley. Sprinkle salmon with salt and pepper and place them on the tray. Rub each fillet with mustard mixture and scatter with walnut mixture; bake for 15 minutes. Drizzle with lemon juice.

Nutrition Info:

- Per Serving: Calories: 300;Fat: 16g;Protein: 17g;-Carbs: 22g.

Sicilian-style Squid With Zucchini

Servings: 4 | Cooking Time: 25 Minutes

Ingredients:

- 2 tbsp olive oil
- 10 oz squid, cut into pieces
- 2 zucchinis, chopped
- 2 tbsp cilantro, chopped
- 1 jalapeno pepper, chopped
- 3 tbsp balsamic vinegar
- Salt and black pepper to taste
- 1 tbsp dill, chopped

Directions:

1. Warm the olive oil in a skillet over medium heat and sauté squid for 5 minutes. Stir in zucchini, cilantro, jalapeño pepper, vinegar, salt, pepper, and dill and cook for another 10 minutes. Serve right away.

Nutrition Info:

- Per Serving: Calories: 240;Fat: 16g;Protein: 12g;-Carbs: 24g.

Better-for-you Cod & Potatoes

Servings: 4 | Cooking Time: 35 Minutes

Ingredients:

- 1 tbsp olive oil
- 2 cod fillets
- 1 tbsp basil, chopped
- Salt and black pepper to taste
- 2 potatoes, peeled and sliced
- 2 tsp turmeric powder
- 1 garlic clove, minced

Directions:

1. Preheat the oven to 360°F. Spread the potatoes on a greased baking dish and season with salt and pepper. Bake for 10 minutes. Arrange the cod fillets on top of the potatoes, sprinkle with salt and pepper, and drizzle with some olive oil. Bake for 10-12 more minutes until the fish flakes easily.
2. Warm the remaining olive oil in a skillet over medium heat and sauté garlic for 1 minute. Stir in basil, salt, pepper, turmeric powder, and 3-4 tbsp of water; cook for another 2-3 minutes. Pour the sauce over the cod fillets and serve warm.

Nutrition Info:

- Per Serving: Calories: 300;Fat: 15g;Protein: 33g;-Carbs: 28g.

Seafood Stew

Servings:4 | Cooking Time:25 Minutes

Ingredients:
- ½ lb skinless trout, cubed
- 2 tbsp olive oil
- ½ lb clams
- ½ lb cod, cubed
- 1 onion, chopped
- ½ fennel bulb, chopped
- 2 garlic cloves, minced
- ¼ cup dry white wine
- 2 tbsp chopped fresh parsley
- 1 can tomato sauce
- 1 cup fish broth
- 1 tbsp Italian seasoning
- ⅛ tsp red pepper flakes
- Salt and black pepper to taste

Directions:

1. Warm olive oil in a pot over medium heat and sauté onion and fennel for 5 minutes. Add in garlic and cook for 30 seconds. Pour in the wine and cook for 1 minute. Stir in tomato sauce, clams, broth, cod, trout, salt, Italian seasoning, red pepper flakes, and pepper. Bring just a boil and simmer for 5 minutes. Discard any unopened clams. Top with parsley.

Nutrition Info:

- Per Serving: Calories: 372;Fat: 15g;Protein: 34g;-Carbs: 25g.

Thyme Hake With Potatoes

Servings:4 | Cooking Time:40 Minutes

Ingredients:
- 1 ½ lb russet potatoes, unpeeled
- ¼ cup olive oil
- ½ tsp garlic powder
- ½ tsp paprika
- Salt and black pepper to taste
- 4 skinless hake fillets
- 4 fresh thyme sprigs
- 1 lemon, sliced

Directions:

1. Preheat oven to 425 °F. Slice the potatoes and toss them with some olive oil, salt, pepper, paprika, and garlic powder in a bowl. Microwave for 12-14 minutes until potatoes are just tender, stirring halfway through microwaving.

2. Transfer the potatoes to a baking dish and press gently into an even layer. Season the hake with salt and pepper, and arrange it skinned side down over the potatoes. Drizzle with the remaining olive oil, then place thyme sprigs and lemon slices on top. Bake for 15-18 minutes until hake flakes apart when gently prodded with a paring knife. Serve and enjoy!

Nutrition Info:

- Per Serving: Calories: 410;Fat: 16g;Protein: 34g;-Carbs: 33g.

Lemon-parsley Swordfish

Servings:4 | Cooking Time: 17 To 20 Minutes

Ingredients:
- 1 cup fresh Italian parsley
- ¼ cup lemon juice
- ¼ cup extra-virgin olive oil
- ¼ cup fresh thyme
- 2 cloves garlic
- ½ teaspoon salt
- 4 swordfish steaks
- Olive oil spray

Directions:

1. Preheat the oven to 450ºF. Grease a large baking dish generously with olive oil spray.
2. Place the parsley, lemon juice, olive oil, thyme, garlic, and salt in a food processor and pulse until smoothly blended.
3. Arrange the swordfish steaks in the greased baking dish and spoon the parsley mixture over the top.
4. Bake in the preheated oven for 17 to 20 minutes until flaky.
5. Divide the fish among four plates and serve hot.

Nutrition Info:
- Per Serving: Calories: 396;Fat: 21.7g;Protein: 44.2g;Carbs: 2.9g.

Parsley Tomato Tilapia

Servings:4 | Cooking Time:20 Minutes

Ingredients:
- 2 tbsp olive oil
- 4 tilapia fillets, boneless
- ½ cup tomato sauce
- 2 tbsp parsley, chopped
- Salt and black pepper to taste

Directions:

1. Warm olive oil in a skillet over medium heat. Sprinkle tilapia with salt and pepper and cook until golden brown, flipping once, about 6 minutes. Pour in the tomato sauce and parsley and cook for an additional 4 minutes. Serve immediately.

Nutrition Info:
- Per Serving: Calories: 308;Fat: 17g;Protein: 16g;Carbs: 3g.

Wine-steamed Clams

Servings:4 | Cooking Time:30 Minutes

Ingredients:
- 4 lb clams, scrubbed and debearded
- 3 tbsp butter
- 3 garlic cloves, minced
- ¼ tsp red pepper flakes
- 1 cup dry white wine
- 3 sprigs fresh thyme
- 2 tbsp fresh dill, minced

Directions:

1. Melt the butter in a large saucepan over medium heat and cook garlic and pepper flakes, stirring constantly, until fragrant, about 30 seconds. Stir in wine and thyme sprigs, bring to a boil and cook until wine is slightly reduced, about 1 minute. Stir in clams. Cover the saucepan and simmer for 15-18 minutes. Remove, discard thyme sprigs and any clams that refuse to open. Sprinkle with dill and serve.

Nutrition Info:
- Per Serving: Calories: 326;Fat: 14g;Protein: 36g;Carbs: 12g.

Cod Fettuccine

Servings:4 | Cooking Time:30 Minutes

Ingredients:
- 1 lb cod fillets, cubed
- 16 oz fettuccine
- 3 tbsp olive oil
- 1 onion, finely chopped
- Salt and lemon pepper to taste
- 1 ½ cups heavy cream
- 1 cup Parmesan cheese, grated

Directions:

1. Boil salted water in a pot over medium heat and stir in fettuccine. Cook according to package directions and drain. Heat the olive oil in a large saucepan over medium heat and add the onion. Stir-fry for 3 minutes until tender. Sprinkle cod with salt and lemon pepper and add to saucepan; cook for 4–5 minutes until fish fillets and flakes easily with a fork. Stir in heavy cream for 2 minutes. Add in the pasta, tossing gently to combine. Cook for 3–4 minutes until sauce is slightly thickened. Sprinkle with Parmesan cheese.

Nutrition Info:
- Per Serving: Calories: 431;Fat: 36g;Protein: 42g;Carbs: 97g.

Grilled Sardines With Herby Sauce

Servings: 4 | Cooking Time: 15 Min + Marinating Time

Ingredients:
- 12 sardines, gutted and cleaned
- 1 lemon, cut into wedges
- 2 garlic cloves, minced
- 2 tbsp capers, finely chopped
- 1 tbsp whole capers
- 1 shallot, diced
- 1 tsp anchovy paste
- 1 lemon, zested and juiced
- 2 tbsp olive oil
- 1 tbsp parsley, finely chopped
- 1 tbsp basil, finely chopped

Directions:

1. In a bowl, blend garlic, chopped capers, shallot, anchovy paste, lemon zest, and olive oil. Add the sardines and toss to coat; let them sit to marinate for about 30 minutes.
2. Preheat your grill to high. Place the sardines on the grill. Cook for 3-4 minutes per side until the skin is browned and beginning to blister. Pour the marinade in a saucepan over medium heat and add the whole capers, parsley, basil, and lemon juice. Cook for 2-3 minutes until thickens. Pour the sauce over grilled sardines. Serve with lemon wedges.

Nutrition Info:
- Per Serving: Calories: 395;Fat: 21g;Protein: 46g;Carbs: 2.1g.

Easy Tomato Tuna Melts

Servings: 2 | Cooking Time: 3 To 4 Minutes

Ingredients:
- 1 can chunk light tuna packed in water, drained
- 2 tablespoons plain Greek yogurt
- 2 tablespoons finely chopped celery
- 1 tablespoon finely chopped red onion
- 2 teaspoons freshly squeezed lemon juice
- Pinch cayenne pepper
- 1 large tomato, cut into ¾-inch-thick rounds
- ½ cup shredded Cheddar cheese

Directions:

1. Preheat the broiler to High.
2. Stir together the tuna, yogurt, celery, red onion, lemon juice, and cayenne pepper in a medium bowl.
3. Place the tomato rounds on a baking sheet. Top each with some tuna salad and Cheddar cheese.
4. Broil for 3 to 4 minutes until the cheese is melted and bubbly. Cool for 5 minutes before serving.

Nutrition Info:
- Per Serving: Calories: 244;Fat: 10.0g;Protein: 30.1g;Carbs: 6.9g.

Balsamic-honey Glazed Salmon

Servings: 4 | Cooking Time: 8 Minutes

Ingredients:

- ½ cup balsamic vinegar
- 1 tablespoon honey
- 4 salmon fillets
- Sea salt and freshly ground pepper, to taste
- 1 tablespoon olive oil

Directions:

1. Heat a skillet over medium-high heat. Combine the vinegar and honey in a small bowl.
2. Season the salmon fillets with the sea salt and freshly ground pepper; brush with the honey-balsamic glaze.
3. Add olive oil to the skillet, and sear the salmon fillets, cooking for 3 to 4 minutes on each side until lightly browned and medium rare in the center.
4. Let sit for 5 minutes before serving.

Nutrition Info:

- Per Serving: Calories: 454;Fat: 17.3g;Protein: 65.3g;Carbs: 9.7g.

Salmon Packets

Servings: 4 | Cooking Time: 25 Minutes

Ingredients:

- 2 tbsp olive oil
- ½ cup apple juice
- 4 salmon fillets
- 4 tsp lemon zest
- 4 tbsp chopped parsley
- Salt and black pepper to taste

Directions:

1. Preheat oven to 380°F. Brush salmon with olive oil and season with salt and pepper. Cut four pieces of nonstick baking paper and divide the salmon between them. Top each one with apple juice, lemon zest, and parsley.
2. Wrap the paper to make packets and arrange them on a baking sheet. Cook for 15 minutes until the salmon is cooked through. Remove the packets to a serving plate, open them, and drizzle with cooking juices to serve.

Nutrition Info:

- Per Serving: Calories: 495;Fat: 21g;Protein: 55g;-Carbs: 5g.

Poultry And Meats Recipes

Poultry And Meats Recipes

Tangy Mushroom & Chicken Kabobs

Servings:4 | Cooking Time:50 Minutes

Ingredients:
- 1 red bell pepper, cut into squares
- 2 tbsp olive oil
- 2 chicken breasts, cubed
- 1 red onion, cut into squares
- 1 cup mushrooms, quartered
- 2 tsp sweet paprika
- 1 tsp ground nutmeg
- 1 tsp Italian seasoning
- ¼ tsp smoked paprika
- Salt and black pepper to taste
- ¼ tsp ground cardamom
- 1 lemon, juiced
- 3 garlic cloves, minced

Directions:
1. Combine chicken, onion, mushrooms, bell pepper, smoked paprika, nutmeg, Italian seasoning, sweet paprika, salt, pepper, cardamom, lemon juice, garlic, and olive oil in a bowl. Transfer to the fridge covered for 30 minutes.
2. Preheat your grill to high. Alternate chicken cubes, peppers, mushrooms, and onions on each of 8 metal skewers. Grill them for 16 minutes on all sides, turning frequently. Serve.

Nutrition Info:
- Per Serving: Calories: 270;Fat: 15g;Protein: 21g;Carbs: 15g.

Roasted Pork Tenderloin With Apple Sauce

Servings:4 | Cooking Time:35 Minutes

Ingredients:
- 2 tbsp olive oil
- 1 lb pork tenderloin
- Salt and black pepper to taste
- ¼ cup apple jelly
- ¼ cup apple juice
- 2 tbsp wholegrain mustard
- 3 sprigs fresh thyme
- ½ tbsp cornstarch
- ½ tbsp heavy cream

Directions:
1. Preheat oven to 330° F. Warm the oil in a skillet over medium heat. Season the pork with salt and pepper. Sear it for 6-8 minutes on all sides. Transfer to a baking sheet. To the same skillet, add the apple jelly, juice, and mustard and stir for 5 minutes over low heat, stirring often. Top with the pork and thyme sprigs. Place the skillet in the oven and bake for 15-18 minutes, brushing the pork with the apple-mustard sauce every 5 minutes. Remove the pork and let it rest for 15 minutes. Place a small pot over low heat. Blend the cornstarch with heavy cream and cooking juices and pour the mixture into the pot. Stir for 2 minutes until thickens. Drizzle the sauce over the pork. Serve sliced and enjoy!

Nutrition Info:
- Per Serving: Calories: 146;Fat: 7g;Protein: 13g;Carbs: 8g.

Homemade Pizza Burgers

Servings:4 | Cooking Time:20 Minutes

Ingredients:

- ¼ tsp mustard powder
- ¼ tsp cumin
- 1 ¼ lb ground beef
- ½ tsp garlic salt
- ¼ tsp red pepper flakes
- ½ tsp Italian seasoning
- 1 cup passata
- 8 mozzarella cheese slices

Directions:

1. Preheat your grill to medium. In a large bowl, lightly mix with your hands the ground beef, mustard powder, cumin, garlic salt, pepper flakes, and Italian seasoning. Shape the mixture into 4 patties. Grill the burgers for about 10 minutes, turning them occasionally to ensure even cooking. In the last 2 minutes of cooking, top each burger with a generous tablespoon of passata and 2 slices of cheese per burger. Remove and let sit for 1–2 minutes before serving.

Nutrition Info:

- Per Serving: Calories: 556;Fat: 39g;Protein: 41g;-Carbs: 8g.

Chicken Drumsticks With Peach Glaze

Servings:4 | Cooking Time:35 Minutes

Ingredients:

- 2 tbsp olive oil
- 8 chicken drumsticks, skinless
- 3 peaches, peeled and chopped
- ¼ cup honey
- ¼ cup cider vinegar
- 1 sweet onion, chopped
- 1 tsp minced fresh rosemary
- Salt to taste

Directions:

1. Warm the olive oil in a large skillet over medium heat. Sprinkle chicken with salt and pepper and brown it for about 7 minutes per side. Remove to a plate. Add onion and rosemary to the skillet and sauté for 1 minute or until lightly golden. Add honey, vinegar, salt, and peaches and cook for 10-12 minutes or until peaches are softened. Add the chicken back to the skillet and heat just until warm, brushing with the sauce. Serve chicken thighs with peach sauce. Enjoy!

Nutrition Info:

- Per Serving: Calories: 1492;Fat: 26g;Protein: 54g;-Carbs: 27g.

Beef & Bell Pepper Bake

Servings:4 | Cooking Time:1 Hour 40 Minutes

Ingredients:

- 2 tbsp olive oil
- 1 lb beef steaks
- 1 red bell pepper, sliced
- 1 green bell pepper, sliced
- 1 yellow bell pepper, sliced
- 2 tbsp oregano, chopped
- 4 garlic cloves, minced
- ½ cup chicken stock
- Salt and black pepper to taste

Directions:

1. Preheat oven to 360° F. Warm olive oil in a skillet over medium heat. Sear the beef steaks for 8 minutes on both sides. Stir in bell peppers, oregano, garlic, stock, salt, and pepper and bake for 80 minutes. Serve warm.

Nutrition Info:

- Per Serving: Calories: 310;Fat: 15g;Protein: 25g;-Carbs: 17g.

Marsala Chicken Cacciatore Stir-fry

Servings:4 | Cooking Time:20 Minutes

Ingredients:

- 3 tbsp olive oil
- 1 lb chicken thigh strips
- ¼ cup Marsala white wine
- 1 tsp dried oregano
- Salt and black pepper to taste
- 2 tsp cornstarch
- 3 tbsp chicken broth
- 1 tomato, chopped
- 1 shallot, chopped
- 1 garlic clove, minced
- ¼ lb mushrooms, sliced
- 1 red bell pepper, sliced
- 2 fresh rosemary sprigs

Directions:

1. In a bowl, combine 2 tbsp of the wine, oregano, salt, pepper, and cornstarch. Add the chicken and toss to coat; set aside. Warm the olive oil in a skillet over medium heat and stir-fry the shallot and garlic for 1 minute until softened. Add the mushrooms and red bell pepper and sauté for 2-3 minutes until lightly tender. Remove to a plate.
2. Brown the chicken in the same skillet for about 5 minutes until it turns white and is nearly cooked through. Pour in the white wine, broth, and tomato mixture while stir-frying. Bring to a boil. Add the vegetables back to the skillet. Cook, stirring, for another 2 minutes to mix everything together. Garnish with rosemary sprigs before serving.

Nutrition Info:

- Per Serving: Calories: 369;Fat: 29g;Protein: 20g;-Carbs: 6g.

Chicken Thighs Al Orange

Servings:4 | Cooking Time:40 Minutes

Ingredients:

- 2 tbsp olive oil
- 2 tbsp sweet chili sauce
- 2 lb chicken thighs, cubed
- Salt and black pepper to taste
- 1 ½ tsp orange extract
- ¼ cup orange juice
- 2 tbsp cilantro, chopped
- 1 cup chicken stock
- ¼ tsp red pepper flakes
- 2 cups cooked white rice

Directions:

1. Warm the olive oil in a skillet over medium heat and sear chicken for 8 minutes on all sides. Season with salt and pepper and stir in orange extract, orange juice, stock, sweet chili sauce, and red pepper flakes. Bring to a boil. Cook for 20 minutes. Top with cilantro and serve over cooked rice.

Nutrition Info:

- Per Serving: Calories: 310;Fat: 15g;Protein: 26g;-Carbs: 23g.

Saucy Turkey With Ricotta Cheese

Servings:4 | Cooking Time:60 Minutes

Ingredients:

- 2 tbsp olive oil
- 1 turkey breast, cubed
- 1 ½ cups salsa verde
- Salt and black pepper to taste
- 4 oz ricotta cheese, crumbled
- 2 tbsp cilantro, chopped

Directions:

1. Preheat the oven to 380° F. Grease a roasting pan with oil. In a bowl, place turkey, salsa verde, salt, and pepper and toss to coat. Transfer to the roasting pan and bake for 50 minutes. Top with ricotta cheese and cilantro and serve.

Nutrition Info:

- Per Serving: Calories: 340;Fat: 16g;Protein: 35g;-Carbs: 23g.

Beef Filet Mignon In Mushroom Sauce

Servings: 2 | **Cooking Time:** 25 Minutes

Ingredients:
- 8 oz cremini mushrooms, quartered
- 2 tbsp olive oil
- 2 filet mignon steaks
- 1 shallot, minced
- 2 tsp flour
- 2 tsp tomato paste
- ½ cup red wine
- 1 cup chicken stock
- ½ tsp dried thyme
- 1 fresh rosemary sprig
- 1 tsp herbes de Provence
- Salt and black pepper to taste
- ¼ tsp garlic powder
- ¼ tsp shallot powder
- ¼ tsp mustard powder

Directions:

1. Warm 1 tablespoon of olive oil in a saucepan over medium heat. Add the mushrooms and shallot and stir-fry for 5-8 minutes. Stir in the flour and tomato paste and cook for another 30 seconds. Pour in the wine and scrape up any browned bits from the sauté pan. Add the chicken stock, thyme, and rosemary. Bring it to a boil and cook until the sauce thickens, 2-4 minutes. In a small bowl, mix the herbes de Provence, salt, garlic powder, shallot powder, mustard powder, salt, and pepper. Rub the beef with the herb mixture on both sides. Warm the remaining olive oil in a sauté over medium heat. Sear the beef for 2-3 minutes on each side. Serve topped with mushroom sauce.

Nutrition Info:
- Per Serving: Calories: 385;Fat: 20g;Protein: 25g;-Carbs: 15g.

Chicken Tagine With Vegetables

Servings: 6 | **Cooking Time:** 67 Minutes

Ingredients:
- 1 ½ lb boneless skinless chicken thighs, cut into chunks
- 2 zucchini, sliced into half-moons
- 4 tbsp olive oil
- Salt and black pepper to taste
- 1 small red onion, chopped
- 2 cloves garlic, minced
- 1 red bell pepper, chopped
- 2 tomatoes, chopped
- 1 tbsp harissa paste
- 1 cup water
- 1 cup black olives, halved
- ¼ cup fresh cilantro, chopped

Directions:

1. Warm the olive oil in a large skillet over medium heat. Season the chicken with salt and pepper and brown for 6-8 minutes on all sides. Add the onion, garlic, and bell pepper and sauté for 5 minutes until tender. Stir in harissa paste and tomatoes for 1 minute and pour in 1 cup of water. Bring to a boil and lower the heat to low. Cover and simmer for 35-45 minutes until the chicken is tender and cooked through. Stir in zucchini and olives and continue to cook for 10 minutes until the zucchini is tender. Serve topped with cilantro.

Nutrition Info:
- Per Serving: Calories: 358;Fat: 25g;Protein: 25g;-Carbs: 8g.

Pork Loaf With Colby Cheese

Servings:6 | Cooking Time:90 Minutes

Ingredients:
- 1 red onion, chopped
- 2 garlic cloves, minced
- 2 lb ground pork
- 2 tbsp milk
- ¼ cup Colby cheese, grated
- 1 egg, whisked
- 10 black olives, chopped
- 2 tbsp oregano, chopped
- Salt and black pepper to taste

Directions:

1. Preheat oven to 360° F. Combine the onion, garlic, pork, milk, Colby cheese, egg, olives, oregano, salt, and pepper in a bowl. Press the mixture into a lightly greased loaf pan. Bake for 50-60 minutes. Let cool slightly. Serve sliced.

Nutrition Info:
- Per Serving: Calories: 360;Fat: 24g;Protein: 25g;-Carbs: 18g.

Beef & Pumpkin Stew

Servings:6 | Cooking Time:35 Minutes

Ingredients:
- 2 tbsp canola oil
- 2 lb stew beef, cubed
- 1 cup red wine
- 1 onion, chopped
- 1 tsp garlic powder
- Salt to taste
- 3 whole cloves
- 1 bay leaf
- 3 carrots, chopped
- ½ butternut pumpkin, diced
- 2 tbsp cornstarch
- 3 tbsp water

Directions:

1. Warm oil on Sauté mode. Brown the beef for 5 minutes on each side. Deglaze the pot with wine, scrape the bottom to get rid of any browned beef bits. Add in onion, salt, bay leaf, cloves, and garlic powder. Seal the lid, press Meat/Stew and cook on High for 15 minutes. Release the Pressure quickly. Add in pumpkin and carrots without stirring.

2. Seal the lid and cook on High Pressure for 5 minutes. Release the Pressure quickly. In a bowl, mix water and cornstarch until cornstarch dissolves completely; mix into the stew. Allow the stew to simmer while uncovered on Keep Warm for 5 minutes until you attain the desired thickness.

Nutrition Info:
- Per Serving: Calories: 340;Fat: 14g;Protein: 34g;-Carbs: 12g.

Greek-style Chicken & Vegetable Stir-fry

Servings:4 | Cooking Time:30 Minutes

Ingredients:
- 2 tbsp olive oil
- 1 lb chicken breasts, chopped
- Salt and black pepper to taste
- 2 cloves garlic, minced
- 2 red bell pepper, chopped
- 1 onion, chopped
- ½ lemon, juiced and zested
- ½ cup feta cheese, crumbled
- 2 tbsp fresh dill, chopped

Directions:

1. Warm the olive oil in a skillet over medium heat. Season the chicken with salt and pepper. Add the chicken and sear for about 4 minutes; reserve. Add the onion, garlic, and bell pepper to the same skillet and stir-fry for 6-8 minutes until crisp-tender. Return the chicken to the skillet and sprinkle with lemon zest and juice. Cook for 1 more minute. Sprinkle with feta cheese and dill and remove from the heat. Cover and allow to sit for 2–3 minutes until the cheese melts. Serve.

Nutrition Info:
- Per Serving: Calories: 347;Fat: 22g;Protein: 28g;-Carbs: 10g.

Eggplant & Turkey Moussaka

Servings:4 | Cooking Time:55 Minutes

Ingredients:
- 5 tbsp olive oil
- 1 lb ground turkey
- 1 can diced tomatoes
- 1 cup Greek yogurt
- 2 small eggplants, sliced
- 2 shallots, chopped
- 2 garlic cloves, minced
- 2 tbsp tomato paste
- 1 tsp dried oregano
- 1 egg, beaten
- Salt and black pepper to taste
- ¼ tsp ground coriander
- 2 oz grated Halloumi cheese
- 2 tbsp chopped fresh parsley

Directions:

1. Preheat oven to 400° F. Warm olive oil in a pan over medium heat and cook the eggplant slices for 6-8 minutes on both sides. Remove to paper towels. In the same pan, sauté shallots and garlic for 3 minutes, stirring often. Add in ground turkey and cook for 5 minutes until no longer pink. Stir in tomato paste, tomatoes, oregano, ground coriander, salt, and pepper; cook for 4-5 minutes.
2. Combine yogurt, egg, salt, and pepper in a bowl. Spread half of the turkey mixture on a baking dish, add a layer of eggplant, then remaining meat, and finally remaining eggplants. Bake for 15 minutes. Remove and top with the yogurt mixture. Sprinkle with the cheese and return in the oven for 5-8 minutes until the cheese melts. Top with parsley.

Nutrition Info:
- Per Serving: Calories: 521;Fat: 33g;Protein: 42g;-Carbs: 23g.

Roasted Herby Chicken

Servings:4 | Cooking Time:80 Minutes

Ingredients:
- 2 tbsp butter, melted
- 1 chicken
- 2 lemons, halved
- 4 rosemary sprigs
- 1 bay leaf
- 6 thyme sprigs
- 1 tsp lemon juice
- Salt and black pepper to taste

Directions:

1. Preheat oven to 420°F and fit a rack into a roasting tray. Brush the chicken with butter on all sides. Put the lemons, herbs, and bay leaf inside the cavity. Drizzle with lemon juice and sprinkle with salt and pepper. Roast for 60-65 minutes. Let rest for 10 minutes before carving.

Nutrition Info:
- Per Serving: Calories: 235;Fat: 7g;Protein: 32g;-Carbs: 2g.

Tzatziki Chicken Loaf

Servings:4 | Cooking Time:70 Min + Chilling Time

Ingredients:
- 1 lb ground chicken
- 1 onion, chopped
- 1 tsp garlic powder
- 1 cup tzatziki sauce
- ½ tsp dried Greek oregano
- ½ tsp dried cilantro
- ½ tsp sweet paprika
- Salt and black pepper to taste

Directions:

1. Preheat oven to 350° F. In a bowl, add chicken, paprika, onion, Greek oregano, cilantro, garlic, salt, and pepper and mix well with your hands. Shape the mixture into a greased loaf pan and bake in the oven for 55-60 minutes. Let sit for 15 minutes and slice. Serve topped with tzatziki sauce.

Nutrition Info:
- Per Serving: Calories: 240;Fat: 9g;Protein: 33.2g;-Carbs: 3.6g.

Eggplant & Chicken Skillet

Servings:4 | Cooking Time:40 Minutes

Ingredients:
- 2 tbsp olive oil
- 1 lb eggplants, cubed
- Salt and black pepper to taste
- 1 onion, chopped
- 2 garlic cloves, minced
- 1 tsp hot paprika
- 1 tbsp oregano, chopped
- 1 cup chicken stock
- 1 lb chicken breasts, cubed
- 1 cup half and half
- 3 tsp toasted chopped almonds

Directions:

1. Warm the olive oil in a skillet over medium heat and sauté chicken for 8 minutes, stirring often. Mix in eggplants, onion, and garlic and cook for another 5 minutes. Season with salt, pepper, hot paprika, and oregano and pour in the stock. Bring to a boil and simmer for 16 minutes. Stir in half and half for 2 minutes. Serve topped with almonds.

Nutrition Info:
- Per Serving: Calories: 400;Fat: 13g;Protein: 26g;-Carbs: 22g.

Chicken Sausages With Pepper Sauce

Servings:4 | Cooking Time:30 Minutes

Ingredients:
- 2 tbsp olive oil
- 4 chicken sausage links
- 2 garlic cloves, minced
- 1 onion, thinly sliced
- 1 red bell pepper, sliced
- 1 green bell pepper, sliced
- ½ cup dry white wine
- Salt and black pepper to taste
- ½ dried chili pepper, minced

Directions:

1. Warm the olive oil in a pan over medium heat and brown the sausages for 6 minutes, turning periodically. Set aside. In the same pan, sauté onion and bell peppers and garlic for 5 minutes until tender. Deglaze with the wine and stir in salt, pepper, and chili pepper. Simmer for 4 minutes until the sauce reduces by half. Serve sausages topped with bell peppers.

Nutrition Info:
- Per Serving: Calories: 193;Fat: 12g;Protein: 6.2g;-Carbs: 10g.

Herby Beef Soup

Servings:4 | Cooking Time:60 Minutes

Ingredients:
- 2 tbsp olive oil
- ½ lb beef stew meat, cubed
- 1 celery stalk, chopped
- 1 tsp fennel seeds
- 1 tsp hot paprika
- 1 carrot, chopped
- 1 onion, chopped
- Salt and black pepper to taste
- 2 garlic cloves, chopped
- 4 cups beef stock
- ½ tsp dried cilantro
- 1 tsp dried oregano
- 14 oz canned tomatoes, diced
- 2 tbsp parsley, chopped

Directions:

1. Warm the olive oil in a pot over medium heat and cook beef meat, onion, and garlic for 10 minutes. Stir in celery, carrots, fennel seeds, paprika, salt, pepper, cilantro, and oregano for 3 minutes. Pour in beef stock and tomatoes and bring to a boil. Cook for 40 minutes. Top with parsley.

Nutrition Info:
- Per Serving: Calories: 350;Fat: 16g;Protein: 38g;-Carbs: 16g.

Beef, Tomato, And Lentils Stew

Servings:4 | Cooking Time: 10 Minutes

Ingredients:
- 1 tablespoon extra-virgin olive oil
- 1 pound extra-lean ground beef
- 1 onion, chopped
- 1 can chopped tomatoes with garlic and basil, drained
- 1 can lentils, drained
- ½ teaspoon sea salt
- ⅛ teaspoon freshly ground black pepper

Directions:

1. Heat the olive oil in a pot over medium-high heat until shimmering.
2. Add the beef and onion to the pot and sauté for 5 minutes or until the beef is lightly browned.
3. Add the remaining ingredients. Bring to a boil. Reduce the heat to medium and cook for 4 more minutes or until the lentils are tender. Keep stirring during the cooking.
4. Pour them in a large serving bowl and serve immediately.

Nutrition Info:
- Per Serving: Calories: 460;Fat: 14.8g;Protein: 44.2g;Carbs: 36.9g.

Pork Butt With Leeks

Servings:4 | Cooking Time:1 Hour 40 Minutes

Ingredients:
- 2 lb boneless pork butt roast, cubed
- 3 tbsp olive oil
- Salt and black pepper to taste
- 2 lb leeks, sliced
- 2 garlic cloves, minced
- 1 can diced tomatoes
- 1 cup dry white wine
- ½ cup chicken broth
- 1 bay leaf
- 2 tsp chopped fresh parsley

Directions:

1. Season the pork with salt and pepper. Warm the oil in a saucepan over medium heat. Brown the pork on all sides, about 8 minutes; transfer to a bowl. Add the leeks, salt, and pepper to fat left in saucepan and sauté for 5-7 minutes, stirring occasionally, until softened and lightly browned. Stir in garlic and cook until fragrant, about 30 seconds. Pour in tomatoes and their juice, scraping up any browned bits, and cook until tomato liquid is nearly evaporated, 10-12 minutes.
2. Preheat oven to 325° F. Add the wine, broth, and bay leaf to the saucepan and return the pork with any accumulated juices; bring to a simmer. Cover, transfer to the oven and cook for about 60 minutes until the pork is tender and falls apart when prodded with a fork. Remove and discard the bay leaf. Sprinkle with parsley. Serve and enjoy!

Nutrition Info:
- Per Serving: Calories: 369;Fat: 14g;Protein: 37g;Carbs: 25g.

Easy Pork Souvlaki

Servings:6 | Cooking Time:20 Min + Marinating Time

Ingredients:
- 3 tbsp olive oil
- 1 onion, grated
- 3 garlic cloves, minced
- 1 tsp ground cumin
- Salt and black pepper to taste
- 2 tsp dried oregano
- 2 lb boneless pork butt, cubed
- 2 lemons, cut into wedges

Directions:

1. In a large bowl, whisk the olive oil, onion, garlic, cumin, salt, pepper, and oregano. Add pork and toss to coat. Cover and place in the refrigerator for at least 2 hours or overnight.
2. Preheat your grill to medium-high. Thread the pork cubes onto bamboo skewers. Place the pork on the grill and cook for about 10 minutes on all sides or until the pork is cooked through. Serve with lemon wedges.

Nutrition Info:
- Per Serving: Calories: 279;Fat: 16g;Protein: 29g;Carbs: 5g.

Deluxe Chicken With Yogurt Sauce

Servings:4 | Cooking Time:40 Minutes

Ingredients:
- 2 tbsp olive oil
- 1/3 cup Greek yogurt
- 1 lb chicken breasts, halved
- 2 garlic cloves, minced
- 2 tbsp lemon juice
- 1 tbsp red wine vinegar
- 2 tbsp dill, chopped
- Salt and black pepper to taste

Directions:

1. Preheat the oven to 380° F. In a food processor, blend garlic, lemon juice, vinegar, yogurt, dill, salt, and pepper until smooth. Warm olive oil in a skillet over medium heat. Sear chicken for 6 minutes on both sides. Pour yogurt sauce over chicken and bake for 25 minutes. Serve.

Nutrition Info:
- Per Serving: Calories: 290;Fat: 13g;Protein: 15g;Carbs: 19g.

Chicken Cacciatore

Servings:2 | Cooking Time: 1 Hour And 30 Minutes

Ingredients:
- 1½ pounds bone-in chicken thighs, skin removed and patted dry
- Salt, to taste
- 2 tablespoons olive oil
- ½ large onion, thinly sliced
- 4 ounces baby bella mushrooms, sliced
- 1 red sweet pepper, cut into 1-inch pieces
- 1 can crushed fire-roasted tomatoes
- 1 fresh rosemary sprig
- ½ cup dry red wine
- 1 teaspoon Italian herb seasoning
- ½ teaspoon garlic powder
- 3 tablespoons flour

Directions:

1. Season the chicken thighs with a generous pinch of salt.
2. Heat the olive oil in a Dutch oven over medium-high heat. Add the chicken and brown for 5 minutes per side.
3. Add the onion, mushrooms, and sweet pepper to the Dutch oven and sauté for another 5 minutes.
4. Add the tomatoes, rosemary, wine, Italian seasoning, garlic powder, and salt, stirring well.
5. Bring the mixture to a boil, then reduce the heat to low. Allow to simmer slowly for at least 1 hour, stirring occasionally, or until the chicken is tender and easily pulls away from the bone.
6. Measure out 1 cup of the sauce from the pot and put it into a bowl. Add the flour and whisk well to make a slurry.
7. Increase the heat to medium-high and slowly whisk the slurry into the pot. Stir until it comes to a boil and cook until the sauce is thickened.
8. Remove the chicken from the bones and shred it, and add it back to the sauce before serving, if desired.

Nutrition Info:
- Per Serving: Calories: 520;Fat: 23.1g;Protein: 31.8g;Carbs: 37.0g.

Grilled Chicken Breasts With Italian Sauce

Servings:4 | Cooking Time:25 Min + Marinating Time

Ingredients:
- ½ cup olive oil
- 2 tbsp rosemary, chopped
- 2 tbsp parsley, chopped
- 1 tsp minced garlic
- 1 lemon, zested and juiced
- Salt and black pepper to taste
- 4 chicken breasts
- 2 tsp basil, chopped

Directions:

1. Combine the olive oil, rosemary, garlic, lemon juice, lemon zest, parsley, salt, and pepper in a plastic bag. Add the chicken and shake to coat. Refrigerate for 2 hours.
2. Heat your grill to medium heat. Remove the chicken breasts from the marinade and grill them for 6-8 minutes per side. Pour the marinade into a saucepan, add 2 tbsp of water and simmer for 2-3 minutes until the sauce thickens. Sprinkle with basil and serve the grilled chicken. Enjoy!

Nutrition Info:
- Per Serving: Calories: 449;Fat: 32g;Protein: 38g;Carbs: 2.1g.

Turmeric Green Bean & Chicken Bake

Servings:4 | Cooking Time:35 Minutes

Ingredients:
- 1 lb green beans, trimmed and halved
- 1 lb chicken thighs, boneless and skinless
- 2 tsp turmeric powder
- ½ cup sour cream
- Salt and black pepper to taste
- 1 tbsp lime juice
- 1 tbsp dill, chopped
- 1 tbsp thyme, chopped

Directions:
1. Preheat the oven to 380° F. Place chicken, turmeric, green beans, sour cream, salt, pepper, lime juice, thyme, and dill in a roasting pan and mix well. Bake for 25 minutes. Serve.

Nutrition Info:
- Per Serving: Calories: 280;Fat: 13g;Protein: 15g;-Carbs: 21g.

Asparagus & Chicken Skillet

Servings:4 | Cooking Time:30 Minutes

Ingredients:
- 2 tbsp olive oil
- 1 lb chicken breasts, sliced
- Salt and black pepper to taste
- 1 lb asparagus, chopped
- 6 sundried tomatoes, diced
- 3 tbsp capers, drained
- 2 tbsp lemon juice

Directions:
1. Warm the olive oil in a skillet over medium heat. Cook asparagus, tomatoes, salt, pepper, capers, and lemon juice for 10 minutes. Remove to a bowl. Brown chicken in the same skillet for 8 minutes on both sides. Put veggies back to skillet and cook for another 2-3 minutes. Serve and enjoy!

Nutrition Info:
- Per Serving: Calories: 560;Fat: 29g;Protein: 45g;-Carbs: 34g.

Tender Pork Shoulder

Servings:4 | Cooking Time:2 Hours 10 Minutes

Ingredients:
- 3 tbsp olive oil
- 2 lb pork shoulder
- 1 onion, chopped
- 2 tbsp garlic, minced
- 1 tbsp hot paprika
- 1 tbsp basil, chopped
- 1 cup chicken broth
- Salt and black pepper to taste

Directions:
1. Preheat oven to 350° F. Heat olive oil in a skillet and brown the pork on all sides for about 8-10 minutes; remove to a baking dish. Add onion and garlic to the skillet and sauté for 3 minutes until softened. Stir in hot paprika, salt, and pepper for 1 minute and pour in chicken broth. Transfer to the baking dish, cover with aluminium foil and bake for 90 minutes. Then remove the foil and continue baking for another 20 minutes until browned on top. Let the pork cool for a few minutes, slice, and sprinkle with basil. Serve topped with the cooking juices.

Nutrition Info:
- Per Serving: Calories: 310;Fat: 15g;Protein: 18g;-Carbs: 21g.

Sides, Salads, And Soups Recipes

Sides, Salads, And Soups Recipes

Sun-dried Tomato & Spinach Pasta Salad

Servings:4 | Cooking Time:45 Min + Cooling Time

Ingredients:
- 1 ½ cups farfalle
- 1 cup chopped baby spinach, rinsed and dried
- 8 sun-dried tomatoes, sliced
- 1 carrot, grated
- 2 scallions, thinly sliced
- 1 garlic clove, minced
- 1 dill pickle, diced
- ⅔ cup extra-virgin olive oil
- 1 tbsp red wine vinegar
- 1 tbsp lemon juice
- ½ cup Greek yogurt
- 1 tsp chopped fresh oregano
- Salt and black pepper to taste
- 1 cup feta cheese, crumbled

Directions:

1. Bring a large pot of salted water to a boil, add the farfalle, and cook for 7-9 minutes until al dente. Drain the pasta and set aside to cool. In a large bowl, combine spinach, sun-dried tomatoes, carrot, scallions, garlic, and pickle. Add pasta and toss to combine. In a medium bowl, whisk olive oil, vinegar, lemon juice, yogurt, oregano, pepper, and salt. Add dressing to pasta and toss to coat. Sprinkle with feta cheese and serve.

Nutrition Info:

- Per Serving: Calories: 239;Fat: 14g;Protein: 8g;-Carbs: 20g.

Zesty Asparagus Salad

Servings:4 | Cooking Time:10 Minutes

Ingredients:
- 4 tbsp olive oil
- 1 lb asparagus
- 1 garlic clove, minced
- Salt and black pepper to taste
- 1 tbsp balsamic vinegar
- 1 tbsp lemon zest

Directions:

1. Roast the asparagus in a greased skillet over medium heat for 5-6 minutes, turning once. Season to taste. Toss with garlic, olive oil, lemon zest, and vinegar. Serve.

Nutrition Info:

- Per Serving: Calories: 148;Fat: 13.6g;Protein: 3g;-Carbs: 5.7g.

Cucumber & Tomato Salad With Anchovies

Servings:4 | Cooking Time:10 Minutes

Ingredients:
- 2 tbsp extra virgin olive oil
- 1 tbsp lemon juice
- 4 canned anchovy fillets
- 6 black olives
- ½ head Romaine lettuce, torn
- Salt and black pepper to taste
- 1 cucumber, cubed
- 3 tomatoes, cubed
- 2 spring onions, chopped

Directions:

1. Whisk the olive oil, lemon juice, salt, and pepper in a bowl. Add the cucumber, tomatoes, and spring onions and toss to coat. Top with anchovies and black olives and serve.

Nutrition Info:

- Per Serving: Calories: 113;Fat: 8.5g;Protein: 2.9g;-Carbs: 9g.

Moroccan Spinach & Lentil Soup

Servings:6 | Cooking Time:35 Minutes

Ingredients:
- 3 tsp olive oil
- 1 onion, chopped
- 1 large carrot, chopped
- 3 garlic cloves, sliced
- 1 ½ cups lentils
- 1 cup crushed tomatoes
- 12 oz spinach

Directions:

1. Warm the olive oil and sauté the onion, garlic, and carrot for 3 minutes. Add the lentils, tomatoes, and 6 cups of water and stir. Cook until the lentils are tender, about 15-20 minutes. Add the spinach and stir until wilted, 5 minutes. Serve hot.

Nutrition Info:
- Per Serving: Calories: 422;Fat: 17g;Protein: 22g;-Carbs: 45g.

Orange-honey Glazed Carrots

Servings:2 | Cooking Time: 15 To 20 Minutes

Ingredients:
- ½ pound rainbow carrots, peeled
- 2 tablespoons fresh orange juice
- 1 tablespoon honey
- ½ teaspoon coriander
- Pinch salt

Directions:

1. Preheat the oven to 400ºF.
2. Cut the carrots lengthwise into slices of even thickness and place in a large bowl.
3. Stir together the orange juice, honey, coriander, and salt in a small bowl. Pour the orange juice mixture over the carrots and toss until well coated.
4. Spread the carrots in a baking dish in a single layer. Roast for 15 to 20 minutes until fork-tender.
5. Let cool for 5 minutes before serving.

Nutrition Info:
- Per Serving: Calories: 85;Fat: 0g;Protein: 1.0g;-Carbs: 21.0g.

Grilled Bell Pepper And Anchovy Antipasto

Servings:4 | Cooking Time: 8 Minutes

Ingredients:
- 2 tablespoons extra-virgin olive oil, divided
- 4 medium red bell peppers, quartered, stem and seeds removed
- 6 ounces anchovies in oil, chopped
- 2 tablespoons capers, rinsed and drained
- 1 cup Kalamata olives, pitted
- 1 small shallot, chopped
- Sea salt and freshly ground pepper, to taste

Directions:

1. Heat the grill to medium-high heat. Grease the grill grates with 1 tablespoon of olive oil.
2. Arrange the red bell peppers on the preheated grill grates, then grill for 8 minutes or until charred.
3. Turn off the grill and allow the pepper to cool for 10 minutes.
4. Transfer the charred pepper in a colander. Rinse and peel the peppers under running cold water, then pat dry with paper towels.
5. Cut the peppers into chunks and combine with remaining ingredients in a large bowl. Toss to mix well.
6. Serve immediately.

Nutrition Info:
- Per Serving: Calories: 227;Fat: 14.9g;Protein: 13.9g;Carbs: 9.9g.

Classic Potato Salad With Green Onions

Servings:4 | Cooking Time:25 Minutes

Ingredients:
- 2 ½ lb baby potatoes, halved
- Salt and black pepper to taste
- 1 cup light mayonnaise
- Juice of 1 lemon
- 2 green onions, chopped
- ¼ cup parsley, chopped

Directions:

1. Place potatoes and enough water in a pot over medium heat and bring to a boil. Cook for 12 minutes and drain; set aside.
2. In a bowl, mix mayonnaise, salt, pepper, lemon juice, and green onions. Add in the baby potatoes and toss to coat. Top with parsley and serve immediately.

Nutrition Info:
- Per Serving: Calories: 360;Fat: 20g;Protein: 11g;Carbs: 25g.

Tricolor Summer Salad

Servings:3 | Cooking Time: 0 Minutes

Ingredients:
- ¼ cup while balsamic vinegar
- 2 tablespoons Dijon mustard
- 1 tablespoon sugar
- ½ teaspoon garlic salt
- ½ teaspoon freshly ground black pepper
- ¼ cup extra-virgin olive oil
- 1½ cups chopped orange, yellow, and red tomatoes
- ½ cucumber, peeled and diced
- 1 small red onion, thinly sliced
- ¼ cup crumbled feta (optional)

Directions:

1. In a small bowl, whisk the vinegar, mustard, sugar, pepper, and garlic salt. Then slowly whisk in the olive oil.
2. In a large bowl, add the tomatoes, cucumber, and red onion. Add the dressing. Toss once or twice, and serve with the feta crumbles (if desired) sprinkled on top.

Nutrition Info:
- Per Serving: Calories: 246;Fat: 18.0g;Protein: 1.0g;Carbs: 19.0g.

Brussels Sprout And Apple Slaw

Servings:4 | Cooking Time: 0 Minutes

Ingredients:
- Salad:
- 1 pound Brussels sprouts, stem ends removed and sliced thinly
- 1 apple, cored and sliced thinly
- ½ red onion, sliced thinly
- Dressing:
- 1 teaspoon Dijon mustard
- 2 teaspoons apple cider vinegar
- 1 tablespoon raw honey
- 1 cup plain coconut yogurt
- 1 teaspoon sea salt
- For Garnish:
- ½ cup pomegranate seeds
- ½ cup chopped toasted hazelnuts

Directions:

1. Combine the ingredients for the salad in a large salad bowl, then toss to combine well.
2. Combine the ingredients for the dressing in a small bowl, then stir to mix well.
3. Dressing the salad. Let sit for 30 minutes, then serve with pomegranate seeds and toasted hazelnuts on top.

Nutrition Info:
- Per Serving: Calories: 248;Fat: 11.2g;Protein: 12.7g;Carbs: 29.9g.

Collard Green & Rice Salad

Servings:4 | Cooking Time:10 Minutes

Ingredients:

- 1 tbsp olive oil
- 1 cup white rice
- 10 oz collard greens, torn
- 4 tbsp walnuts, chopped
- 2 tbsp balsamic vinegar
- 4 tbsp tahini paste
- Salt and black pepper to taste
- 2 tbsp parsley, chopped

Directions:

1. Bring to a boil salted water over medium heat. Add in the rice and cook for 15-18 minutes. Drain and rest to cool.
2. Whisk tahini, 4 tbsp of cold water, and vinegar in a bowl. In a separate bowl, combine cooled rice, collard greens, walnuts, salt, pepper, olive oil, and tahini dressing. Serve topped with parsley.

Nutrition Info:

- Per Serving: Calories: 180;Fat: 4g;Protein: 4g;Carbs: 6g.

Zoodles With Tomato-mushroom Sauce

Servings:4 | Cooking Time:25 Minutes

Ingredients:

- 1 lb oyster mushrooms, chopped
- 2 tbsp olive oil
- 1 cup chicken broth
- 1 tsp Mediterranean sauce
- 1 yellow onion, minced
- 1 cup pureed tomatoes
- 2 garlic cloves, minced
- 2 zucchinis, spiralized

Directions:

1. Warm the olive oil in a saucepan over medium heat and sauté the zoodles for 1-2 minutes; reserve. Sauté the onion and garlic in the same saucepan for 2-3 minutes. Add in the mushrooms and continue to cook for 2 to 3 minutes until they release liquid. Add in the remaining ingredients and cover the pan; let it simmer for 10 minutes longer until everything is cooked through. Top the zoodles with the prepared mushroom sauce and serve.

Nutrition Info:

- Per Serving: Calories: 95;Fat: 6.4g;Protein: 6g;Carbs: 5g.

Italian Spinach & Rice Soup

Servings:6 | Cooking Time:65 Minutes

Ingredients:

- 3 tbsp olive oil
- 1 large onion, chopped
- 2 cloves garlic, minced
- 2 lb spinach leaves, chopped
- 6 cups chicken broth
- ½ cup arborio rice
- Salt and black pepper to taste
- 2 oz shaved Parmesan cheese

Directions:

1. Warm the olive oil in a large pot oven over medium heat and add the onion and garlic. Cook until the onions are soft and translucent, about 5 minutes. Add the spinach and stir. Cover the pot and cook the spinach until wilted, about 3 more minutes. With a slotted spoon, remove the spinach and onions from the pot, leaving the liquid.
2. Transfer the spinach mixture to your food processor and process until smooth, then return to the pot. Add the chicken broth and bring to a boil. Add the rice, reduce heat, and simmer until the rice is tender, about 20 minutes. Adjust the taste. Serve topped with Parmesan shavings.

Nutrition Info:

- Per Serving: Calories: 157;Fat: 3.6g;Protein: 8g;Carbs: 27.1g.

Leek & Shrimp Soup

Servings: 6 | Cooking Time: 40 Minutes

Ingredients:
- 1 lb shrimp, peeled and deveined
- 3 tbsp olive oil
- 1 celery stalk, chopped
- 1 leek, sliced
- 1 fennel bulb, chopped
- 2 garlic cloves, minced
- Salt and black pepper to taste
- 1 tbsp coriander seeds
- 6 cups vegetable broth
- 2 tbsp buttermilk
- 1 lemon, juiced

Directions:

1. Warm the oil in a large pot oven over medium heat. Add the celery, leek, and fennel, and cook for about 5 minutes until tender. Add the garlic and season with salt and pepper. Add the coriander seeds and stir. Pour in the broth, bring to a boil, and then reduce to a simmer and cook for 20 more minutes. Add the shrimp to the soup and cook until just pink, about 3 minutes. Stir in buttermilk and lemon juice. Serve.

Nutrition Info:
- Per Serving: Calories: 286; Fat: 9g; Protein: 17g;- Carbs: 34g.

Mascarpone Sweet Potato Mash

Servings: 4 | Cooking Time: 30 Minutes

Ingredients:
- ¼ cup mascarpone cheese, softened
- ¼ cup olive oil
- ½ tsp ground nutmeg
- 1 ¼ lb sweet potatoes, cubed
- Salt and black pepper to taste
- 1 tbsp fresh chives, chopped

Directions:

1. Place the potatoes in a pot over high heat and cover with water. Bring to a boil, then lower the heat and simmer covered for 20 minutes. Drain the potatoes and back to the pot. Stir in mascarpone, olive oil, nutmeg, salt, and pepper. Mash them with a potato masher until smooth. Sprinkle with chives.

Nutrition Info:
- Per Serving: Calories: 304; Fat: 15g; Protein: 4g;- Carbs: 40.2g.

Summer Gazpacho

Servings: 6 | Cooking Time: 15 Minutes

Ingredients:
- ⅓ cup extra-virgin olive oil
- ½ cup of water
- 2 bread slices, torn
- 2 lb ripe tomatoes, seeded
- 1 cucumber, chopped
- 1 clove garlic, finely chopped
- ½ red onion, diced
- 2 tbsp red wine vinegar
- 1 tbsp fresh thyme, chopped
- Salt to taste

Directions:

1. Put the bread in 1 cup of water mixed with 1 tbsp of vinegar and salt to soak for 5 minutes. Then, blend the soaked bread, tomatoes, cucumber, garlic, red onion, olive oil, vinegar, thyme, and salt in your food processor until completely smooth. Pour the soup into a glass container and store in the fridge until chilled. Serve drizzled with olive oil.

Nutrition Info:
- Per Serving: Calories: 163; Fat: 13g; Protein: 2g;- Carbs: 12.4g.

Baby Spinach & Apple Salad With Walnuts

Servings: 4 | Cooking Time: 5 Minutes

Ingredients:
- 2 oz sharp white cheddar cheese, cubed
- 3 tbsp olive oil
- 8 cups baby spinach
- 1 Granny Smith apple, diced
- 1 medium red apple, diced
- ½ cup toasted pecans
- 1 tbsp apple cider vinegar

Directions:

1. Toss the spinach, apples, pecans, and cubed cheese together. Lightly drizzle olive oil and vinegar over the top and serve.

Nutrition Info:
- Per Serving: Calories: 138; Fat: 12.8g; Protein: 1g;- Carbs: 7g.

Greek Chicken, Tomato, And Olive Salad

Servings:2 | Cooking Time: 0 Minutes

Ingredients:

- Salad:
- 2 grilled boneless, skinless chicken breasts, sliced
- 10 cherry tomatoes, halved
- 8 pitted Kalamata olives, halved
- ½ cup thinly sliced red onion
- Dressing:
- ¼ cup balsamic vinegar
- 1 teaspoon freshly squeezed lemon juice
- ¼ teaspoon sea salt
- ¼ teaspoon freshly ground black pepper
- 2 teaspoons extra-virgin olive oil
- For Serving:
- 2 cups roughly chopped romaine lettuce
- ½ cup crumbled feta cheese

Directions:

1. Combine the ingredients for the salad in a large bowl. Toss to combine well.
2. Combine the ingredients for the dressing in a small bowl. Stir to mix well.
3. Pour the dressing the bowl of salad, then toss to coat well. Wrap the bowl in plastic and refrigerate for at least 2 hours.
4. Remove the bowl from the refrigerator. Spread the lettuce on a large plate, then top with marinated salad. Scatter the salad with feta cheese and serve immediately.

Nutrition Info:

- Per Serving: Calories: 328;Fat: 16.9g;Protein: 27.6g;Carbs: 15.9g.

Pine Nut & Raisin Spinach

Servings:4 | Cooking Time:10 Minutes

Ingredients:

- 2 tbsp olive oil
- 4 cups fresh baby spinach
- 1 garlic clove, minced
- 2 tbsp raisins, soaked
- 2 tbsp toasted pine nuts
- Salt and black pepper to taste

Directions:

1. Warm olive oil in a pan over medium heat and sauté spinach and garlic for 3 minutes until the spinach wilts. Mix in raisins, pine nuts, salt, and pepper and cook for 3 minutes.

Nutrition Info:

- Per Serving: Calories: 111;Fat: 10g;Protein: 1.8g;Carbs: 5.5g.

Roasted Cherry Tomato & Fennel

Servings:4 | Cooking Time:35 Minutes

Ingredients:

- ¼ cup olive oil
- 20 cherry tomatoes, halved
- 2 fennel bulbs, cut into wedges
- 10 black olives, sliced
- 1 lemon, cut into wedges
- Salt and black pepper to taste

Directions:

1. Preheat oven to 425° F. Combine fennel, olive oil, tomatoes, salt, and pepper in a bowl. Place in a baking pan and roast in the oven for about 25 minutes until golden. Top with olives and serve with lemon wedges on the side.

Nutrition Info:

- Per Serving: Calories: 268;Fat: 15.2g;Protein: 7g;Carbs: 33g.

Parsley Turkish Chicken Soup

Servings:6 | Cooking Time:40 Minutes

Ingredients:
- 1 tbsp olive oil
- 1 lb chicken breasts, cubed
- Salt and black pepper to taste
- 2 celery stalks, chopped
- 1 carrot, chopped
- 1 red onion, chopped
- 6 cups chicken stock
- ½ cup parsley, chopped
- ½ cup buckwheat
- 1 tsp lime juice
- 1 lime, sliced

Directions:

1. Warm the olive oil in a pot over medium heat. Season chicken breasts with salt and pepper and cook for 8 minutes. Stir in onion, carrot, and celery and sauté for another 3 minutes or until soft and aromatic. Put in chicken stock and buckwheat and bring to a boil. Reduce the heat to low. Let it simmer for about 20 minutes and add in lime juice. Sprinkle with parsley. Ladle your soup into individual bowls and serve warm with gremolata toast and lime slices. Yummy!

Nutrition Info:
- Per Serving: Calories: 320;Fat: 9g;Protein: 24g;Carbs: 18g.

Root Vegetable Roast

Servings:4 | Cooking Time: 25 Minutes

Ingredients:
- 1 bunch beets, peeled and cut into 1-inch cubes
- 2 small sweet potatoes, peeled and cut into 1-inch cubes
- 3 parsnips, peeled and cut into 1-inch rounds
- 4 carrots, peeled and cut into 1-inch rounds
- 1 tablespoon raw honey
- 1 teaspoon sea salt
- ½ teaspoon freshly ground black pepper
- 1 tablespoon extra-virgin olive oil
- 2 tablespoons coconut oil, melted

Directions:

1. Preheat the oven to 400ºF. Line a baking sheet with parchment paper.
2. Combine all the ingredients in a large bowl. Toss to coat the vegetables well.
3. Pour the mixture in the baking sheet, then place the sheet in the preheated oven.
4. Roast for 25 minutes or until the vegetables are lightly browned and soft. Flip the vegetables halfway through the cooking time.
5. Remove the vegetables from the oven and allow to cool before serving.

Nutrition Info:
- Per Serving: Calories: 461;Fat: 18.1g;Protein: 5.9g;Carbs: 74.2g.

Mushroom And Soba Noodle Soup

Servings:4 | Cooking Time: 10 Minutes

Ingredients:
- 2 tablespoons coconut oil
- 8 ounces shiitake mushrooms, stemmed and sliced thin
- 1 tablespoon minced fresh ginger
- 4 scallions, sliced thin
- 1 garlic clove, minced
- 1 teaspoon sea salt
- 4 cups low-sodium vegetable broth
- 3 cups water
- 4 ounces soba noodles
- 1 bunch spinach, blanched, rinsed and cut into strips
- 1 tablespoon freshly squeezed lemon juice

Directions:

1. Heat the coconut oil in a stockpot over medium heat until melted.
2. Add the mushrooms, ginger, scallions, garlic, and salt. Sauté for 5 minutes or until fragrant and the mushrooms are tender.
3. Pour in the vegetable broth and water. Bring to a boil, then add the soba noodles and cook for 5 minutes or until al dente.
4. Turn off the heat and add the spinach and lemon juice. Stir to mix well.
5. Pour the soup in a large bowl and serve immediately.

Nutrition Info:
- Per Serving: Calories: 254;Fat: 9.2g;Protein: 13.1g;Carbs: 33.9g.

Parmesan Roasted Red Potatoes

Servings: 2 | Cooking Time: 55 Minutes

Ingredients:

- 12 ounces red potatoes, scrubbed and diced into 1-inch pieces
- 1 tablespoon olive oil
- ½ teaspoon garlic powder
- ¼ teaspoon salt
- 1 tablespoon grated Parmesan cheese
- 1 teaspoon minced fresh rosemary

Directions:

1. Preheat the oven to 425ºF. Line a baking sheet with parchment paper.
2. In a mixing bowl, combine the potatoes, olive oil, garlic powder, and salt. Toss well to coat.
3. Lay the potatoes on the parchment paper and roast for 10 minutes. Flip the potatoes over and roast for another 10 minutes.
4. Check the potatoes to make sure they are golden brown on the top and bottom. Toss them again, turn the heat down to 350ºF, and roast for 30 minutes more.
5. When the potatoes are golden brown, scatter the Parmesan cheese over them and toss again. Return to the oven for 3 minutes to melt the cheese.
6. Remove from the oven and sprinkle with the fresh rosemary before serving.

Nutrition Info:

- Per Serving: Calories: 200;Fat: 8.2g;Protein: 5.1g;-Carbs: 30.0g.

Classic Aioli

Servings: 6 | Cooking Time: 10 Minutes

Ingredients:

- ½ cup sunseed oil
- 1 garlic clove, minced
- 2 tsp lemon juice
- 1 tsp lemon zest
- 1 large egg yolk
- Salt to taste

Directions:

1. Blitz all the ingredients in a large bowl with an immersion blender until everything is well combined and thick. Store in an airtight container in the refrigerator for up to 2-3 days.

Nutrition Info:

- Per Serving: Calories: 181;Fat: 9.7g;Protein: 3.3g;-Carbs: 4g.

Eggplant Casserole With Pecorino Cheese

Servings: 4 | Cooking Time: 40 Minutes

Ingredients:

- 2 tbsp olive oil
- 1 lb eggplants, sliced
- 1 onion, sliced
- 1 cup tomatoes, sliced
- 4 tbsp Pecorino cheese, grated
- 1 celery stalk, sliced
- 4 garlic cloves, crushed
- 1 tsp Italian seasoning
- 1 chili pepper, minced

Directions:

1. Preheat oven to 360° F. Arrange the vegetables on a greased baking dish and sprinkle with spices and olive oil. Roast the vegetables for 18-20 minutes. Scatter the cheese on the top and continue to bake for a further 10 minutes. Serve warm.

Nutrition Info:

- Per Serving: Calories: 160;Fat: 11g;Protein: 7g;-Carbs: 8g.

Rich Chicken And Small Pasta Broth

Servings:6 | Cooking Time: 4 Hours

Ingredients:
- 6 boneless, skinless chicken thighs
- 4 stalks celery, cut into ½-inch pieces
- 4 carrots, cut into 1-inch pieces
- 1 medium yellow onion, halved
- 2 garlic cloves, minced
- 2 bay leaves
- Sea salt and freshly ground black pepper, to taste
- 6 cups low-sodium chicken stock
- ½ cup stelline pasta
- ¼ cup chopped fresh flat-leaf parsley

Directions:
1. Combine the chicken thighs, celery, carrots, onion, and garlic in the slow cooker. Spread with bay leaves and sprinkle with salt and pepper. Toss to mix well.
2. Pour in the chicken stock. Put the lid on and cook on high for 4 hours or until the internal temperature of chicken reaches at least 165°F.
3. In the last 20 minutes of the cooking, remove the chicken from the slow cooker and transfer to a bowl to cool until ready to reserve.
4. Discard the bay leaves and add the pasta to the slow cooker. Put the lid on and cook for 15 minutes or until al dente.
5. Meanwhile, slice the chicken, then put the chicken and parsley in the slow cooker and cook for 5 minutes or until well combined.
6. Pour the soup in a large bowl and serve immediately.

Nutrition Info:
- Per Serving: Calories: 285;Fat: 10.8g;Protein: 27.4g;Carbs: 18.8g.

Pecorino Zucchini Strips

Servings:4 | Cooking Time:30 Minutes

Ingredients:
- 4 zucchini, quartered lengthwise
- 2 tbsp olive oil
- ½ cup grated Pecorino cheese
- 1 tbsp dried dill
- ¼ tsp garlic powder
- Salt and black pepper to taste

Directions:
1. Preheat oven to 350° F. Combine zucchini and olive oil in a bowl. Mix cheese, salt, garlic powder, dill, and pepper in a bowl. Add in zucchini and toss to combine. Arrange the zucchini fingers on a lined baking sheet and bake for about 20 minutes until golden Set oven to broil and broil for 2 minutes until crispy. Serve and enjoy!

Nutrition Info:
- Per Serving: Calories: 103;Fat: 8.2g;Protein: 3.5g;Carbs: 6g.

Green Beans With Tahini-lemon Sauce

Servings:2 | Cooking Time: 10 Minutes

Ingredients:
- 1 pound green beans, washed and trimmed
- 2 tablespoons tahini
- 1 garlic clove, minced
- Grated zest and juice of 1 lemon
- Salt and black pepper, to taste
- 1 teaspoon toasted black or white sesame seeds (optional)

Directions:
1. Steam the beans in a medium saucepan fitted with a steamer basket (or by adding ¼ cup water to a covered saucepan) over medium-high heat. Drain, reserving the cooking water.
2. Mix the tahini, garlic, lemon zest and juice, and salt and pepper to taste. Use the reserved cooking water to thin the sauce as desired.
3. Toss the green beans with the sauce and garnish with the sesame seeds, if desired. Serve immediately.

Nutrition Info:
- Per Serving: Calories: 188;Fat: 8.4g;Protein: 7.2g;Carbs: 22.2g.

Beans, Grains, And Pastas Recipes

Beans, Grains, And Pastas Recipes

Easy Walnut And Ricotta Spaghetti

Servings:6 | Cooking Time: 10 Minutes

Ingredients:

- 1 pound cooked whole-wheat spaghetti
- 2 tablespoons extra-virgin olive oil
- 4 cloves garlic, minced
- ¾ cup walnuts, toasted and finely chopped
- 2 tablespoons ricotta cheese
- ¼ cup flat-leaf parsley, chopped
- ½ cup grated Parmesan cheese
- Sea salt and freshly ground pepper, to taste

Directions:

1. Reserve a cup of spaghetti water while cooking the spaghetti.
2. Heat the olive oil in a nonstick skillet over medium-low heat or until shimmering.
3. Add the garlic and sauté for a minute or until fragrant.
4. Pour the spaghetti water into the skillet and cook for 8 more minutes.
5. Turn off the heat and mix in the walnuts and ricotta cheese.
6. Put the cooked spaghetti on a large serving plate, then pour the walnut sauce over. Spread with parsley and Parmesan, then sprinkle with salt and ground pepper. Toss to serve.

Nutrition Info:

- Per Serving: Calories: 264;Fat: 16.8g;Protein: 8.6g;-Carbs: 22.8g.

Sweet Potatoes Stuffed With Beans

Servings:4 | Cooking Time:50 Minutes

Ingredients:

- 4 sweet potatoes, pierced with a fork
- 2 tbsp olive oil
- 1 cup canned cannellini beans
- 1 small red pepper, chopped
- 1 tbsp lemon zest
- 2 tbsp lemon juice
- 1 garlic clove, minced
- 1 tbsp oregano, chopped
- 1 tbsp parsley, chopped
- Salt and black pepper to taste
- 1 avocado, mashed
- 1 tbsp tahini paste

Directions:

1. Preheat oven to 360° F. Line a baking sheet with parchment paper and place in the sweet potatoes. Bake for 40 minutes. Let cool and cut in half. Using a spoon, remove some flesh of the potatoes and place it in a bowl. Mix in beans, red pepper, lemon zest, half of the lemon juice, half of the oil, half of the garlic, oregano, half of the parsley, salt, and pepper.
2. Divide the mixture between the potato halves. In another bowl, combine avocado, 2 tbsp of water, tahini, remaining lemon juice, remaining oil, remaining garlic, and remaining parsley and scatter over stuffed potatoes. Serve chilled.

Nutrition Info:

- Per Serving: Calories: 303;Fat: 3g;Protein: 8g;Carbs: 40g.

Raspberry & Nut Quinoa

Servings:4 | Cooking Time:5 Minutes

Ingredients:

- 1 tbsp honey
- 2 cups almond milk
- 2 cups quinoa, cooked
- ½ tsp cinnamon powder
- 1 cup raspberries
- ¼ cup walnuts, chopped

Directions:

1. Combine quinoa, milk, cinnamon powder, honey, raspberries, and walnuts in a bowl. Serve in individual bowls.

Nutrition Info:

- Per Serving: Calories: 300;Fat: 15g;Protein: 5g;-Carbs: 15g.

Spinach Farfalle With Ricotta Cheese

Servings:4 | Cooking Time:25 Minutes

Ingredients:

- ¼ cup extra-virgin olive oil
- ½ cup crumbled ricotta cheese
- 2 tbsp black olives, halved
- 4 cups fresh baby spinach, chopped
- 2 tbsp scallions, chopped
- 16 oz farfalle pasta
- ¼ cup red wine vinegar
- 2 tsp lemon juice
- Salt and black pepper to taste

Directions:

1. Cook the farfalle pasta to pack instructions, drain and let it to cool. Mix the scallions, spinach, and cooled pasta in a bowl. Top with ricotta and olives. Combine the vinegar, olive oil, lemon juice, salt, and pepper in another bowl. Pour over the pasta mixture and toss to combine. Serve chilled.

Nutrition Info:

- Per Serving: Calories: 377;Fat: 16g;Protein: 12g;-Carbs: 44g.

Tomato Sauce And Basil Pesto Fettuccine

Servings:4 | Cooking Time: 15 Minutes

Ingredients:

- 4 Roma tomatoes, diced
- 2 teaspoons no-salt-added tomato paste
- 1 tablespoon chopped fresh oregano
- 2 garlic cloves, minced
- 1 cup low-sodium vegetable soup
- ½ teaspoon sea salt
- 1 packed cup fresh basil leaves
- ¼ cup pine nuts
- ¼ cup grated Parmesan cheese
- 2 tablespoons extra-virgin olive oil
- 1 pound cooked whole-grain fettuccine

Directions:

1. Put the tomatoes, tomato paste, oregano, garlic, vegetable soup, and salt in a skillet. Stir to mix well.
2. Cook over medium heat for 10 minutes or until lightly thickened.
3. Put the remaining ingredients, except for the fettuccine, in a food processor and pulse to combine until smooth.
4. Pour the puréed basil mixture into the tomato mixture, then add the fettuccine. Cook for a few minutes or until heated through and the fettuccine is well coated.
5. Serve immediately.

Nutrition Info:

- Per Serving: Calories: 389;Fat: 22.7g;Protein: 9.7g;-Carbs: 40.2g.

Paprika Spinach & Chickpea Bowl

Servings:4 | Cooking Time:20 Minutes

Ingredients:
- 2 tbsp olive oil
- 1 lb canned chickpeas
- 10 oz spinach
- 1 tsp coriander seeds
- 1 red onion, finely chopped
- 2 tomatoes, pureed
- 1 garlic clove, minced
- ½ tbsp rosemary
- ½ tsp smoked paprika
- Salt and white pepper to taste

Directions:
1. Heat the olive oil in a pot over medium heat. Add in the onion, garlic, coriander seeds, salt, and pepper and cook for 3 minutes until translucent. Stir in tomatoes, rosemary, paprika, salt, and white pepper. Bring to a boil, then lower the heat, and simmer for 10 minutes. Add in chickpeas and spinach and cook covered until the spinach wilts. Serve.

Nutrition Info:
- Per Serving: Calories: 512;Fat: 1.8g;Protein: 25g;-Carbs: 76g.

Parmesan Beef Rotini With Asparagus

Servings:4 | Cooking Time:40 Minutes

Ingredients:
- 1 lb asparagus, cut into 1-inch pieces
- 3 tbsp olive oil
- 16 oz rotini pasta
- 1 lb ground beef
- 2 large shallots, chopped
- 3 garlic cloves, minced
- Salt and black pepper to taste
- 1 cup grated Parmesan cheese

Directions:
1. In a pot of boiling water, cook the rotini pasta for 8-10 minutes until al dente. Drain and set aside.
2. Heat a large non-stick skillet over medium heat and add the beef. Cook while breaking the lumps that form until brown, 10 minutes. Use a slotted spoon to transfer the beef to a plate and discard the drippings. Heat olive oil in a skillet and sauté asparagus until tender, 7 minutes. Stir in shallots and garlic and cook for 2 minutes. Season with salt and pepper. Stir in the beef and rotini pasta and toss until well combined. Adjust the taste with salt and black pepper as desired. Dish the food between serving plates and garnish with Parmesan.

Nutrition Info:
- Per Serving: Calories: 513;Fat: 25g;Protein: 44g;-Carbs: 21g.

Cranberry & Walnut Freekeh Pilaf

Servings:4 | Cooking Time:30 Minutes

Ingredients:
- 2 tbsp olive oil
- 2 ½ cups freekeh, soaked
- 2 medium onions, diced
- ¼ tsp ground cinnamon
- ¼ tsp ground allspice
- ¼ tsp ground nutmeg
- 5 cups chicken stock
- ½ cup walnuts, chopped
- Salt and black pepper to taste
- ½ cup Greek yogurt
- 1 ½ tsp lemon juice
- ½ tsp garlic powder
- 1 tbsp dried cranberries

Directions:
1. Warm the olive oil in a large skillet over medium heat and sauté the onions and cook until fragrant. Add the freekeh, cinnamon, nutmeg, and allspice. Stir for 1 minute. Pour in the stock, cranberries, and walnuts and season with salt and pepper. Bring to a simmer. Cover and reduce the heat to low.
2. Simmer for 15 minutes until the freekeh is tender. Remove from the heat and leave to sit for 5 minutes. In a small bowl, mix the yogurt, lemon juice, and garlic powder. Add the yogurt mixture to the freekeh and serve immediately.

Nutrition Info:
- Per Serving: Calories: 650;Fat: 25g;Protein: 12g;-Carbs: 91g.

Valencian-style Mussel Rice

Servings: 4 | Cooking Time: 40 Minutes

Ingredients:
- 1 lb mussels, cleaned and debearded
- 2 tbsp olive oil
- 2 garlic cloves, minced
- 1 yellow onion, chopped
- 2 tomatoes, chopped
- 2 cups fish stock
- 1 cup white rice
- 1 bunch parsley, chopped
- Salt and white pepper to taste

Directions:

1. Warm the olive oil in a pot over medium heat and cook onion and garlic for 5 minutes. Stir in rice for 1 minute. Pour in tomatoes and fish stock and bring to a boil. Add in the mussels and simmer for 20 minutes. Discard any unopened mussels. Adjust the taste with salt and white pepper. Serve topped with parsley.

Nutrition Info:
- Per Serving: Calories: 310;Fat: 15g;Protein: 12g;-Carbs: 17g.

Florentine Bean & Vegetable Gratin

Servings: 4 | Cooking Time: 50 Minutes

Ingredients:
- ½ cup Parmigiano Reggiano cheese, grated
- 4 pancetta slices
- 2 tbsp olive oil
- 4 garlic cloves, minced
- 1 onion, chopped
- ½ fennel bulb, chopped
- 1 tbsp brown rice flour
- 2 cans white beans
- 1 can tomatoes, diced
- 1 medium zucchini, chopped
- 1 tsp porcini powder
- 1 tbsp fresh basil, chopped
- ½ tsp dried oregano
- 1 tsp red pepper flakes
- Salt to taste
- 2 tbsp butter, cubed

Directions:

1. Heat the olive in a skillet over medium heat. Fry the pancetta for 5 minutes until crispy. Drain on paper towels, chop, and reserve. Add garlic, onion, and fennel to the skillet and sauté for 5 minutes until softened. Stir in rice flour for 3 minutes.

2. Preheat oven to 350° F. Add the beans, tomatoes, and zucchini to a casserole dish and pour in the sautéed vegetable and chopped pancetta; mix well. Sprinkle with porcini powder, oregano, red pepper flakes, and salt. Top with Parmigiano Reggiano cheese and butter and bake for 25 minutes or until the cheese is lightly browned. Garnish with basil and serve.

Nutrition Info:
- Per Serving: Calories: 483;Fat: 28g;Protein: 19g;-Carbs: 42g.

Spanish-style Linguine With Tapenade

Servings: 4 | Cooking Time: 20 Minutes

Ingredients:
- 1 cup black olives, pitted
- 2 tbsp capers
- 2 tbsp rosemary, chopped
- 1 garlic clove, smashed
- 2 anchovy fillets, chopped
- ½ tsp sugar
- ⅔ cup + 2 tbsp olive oil
- 1 lb linguine
- ½ cup grated Manchego cheese
- 1 tbsp chopped fresh chives

Directions:

1. Process the olives, capers, rosemary, garlic, anchovies, sugar, and ⅔ cup olive oil in your food processor until well incorporated but not smooth; set aside. Bring a large pot of salted water to a boil, add the linguine, and cook for 7-9 minutes until al dente. Drain the pasta in a bowl and add the remaining 2 tablespoons olive oil and Manchego cheese; toss to coat. Arrange pasta on a serving platter and top it with tapenade and chives. Serve and enjoy!

Nutrition Info:
- Per Serving: Calories: 375;Fat: 39g;Protein: 5g;-Carbs: 23g.

Green Pea & Cavolo Nero Farro Pilaf

Servings:4 | Cooking Time:50 Minutes

Ingredients:
- 2 tbsp olive oil
- 1 cup green peas
- 4 cups cavolo nero, torn
- ½ cup hummus
- ½ cup scallions, sliced
- 1 garlic clove, minced
- 1 cup farro
- 2 cups water
- 1 cup chopped tomatoes
- 1 tbsp tomato paste
- 1 tsp cumin
- ½ tsp oregano
- 2 tbsp fresh cilantro, chopped
- Salt and black pepper to taste

Directions:

1. Heat the olive oil in a skillet over medium heat. Add in scallions, sauté until tender. Add in garlic, cumin, and oregano and cook for another 30 seconds. Stir in farro, water, chopped tomatoes, and tomato paste. Bring to a boil, then lower the heat, and simmer for 30-40 minutes. Stir in peas, cavolo nero, salt, and black pepper. Let sit covered for 8 minutes. Serve topped with hummus and cilantro.

Nutrition Info:
- Per Serving: Calories: 362;Fat: 11g;Protein: 10g;-Carbs: 57g.

Bolognese Penne Bake

Servings:6 | Cooking Time:55 Minutes

Ingredients:
- 1 lb penne pasta
- 1 lb ground beef
- A pinch of two salt
- 1 basil-tomato sauce
- 1 lb baby spinach, washed
- 3 cups mozzarella, shredded

Directions:

1. Bring a pot of salted water to a boil, add the pasta, and cook until al dente. Reserve 1 cup of the pasta water; drain the pasta.
2. Preheat the oven to 350°F. In a skillet over medium heat, stir-fry the ground beef along with a pinch of salt until browned, 5 minutes. Stir in basil-tomato sauce and 2 cups of pasta water and let simmer for 5 minutes. Add a handful of spinach, one at a time, into the sauce, and cook for 3 minutes.
3. In a large baking dish, add the pasta and pour the sauce over it. Stir in 1 ½ cups of mozzarella cheese, cover the dish with aluminum foil and bake for 20 minutes. After 20 minutes, remove the foil, top with the remaining mozzarella, and bake for another 8-12 minutes until golden brown. Serve.

Nutrition Info:
- Per Serving: Calories: 445;Fat: 21g;Protein: 29g;-Carbs: 43g.

Ricotta & Olive Rigatoni

Servings:4 | Cooking Time:25 Minutes

Ingredients:
- 2 tbsp extra-virgin olive oil
- 1 lb rigatoni
- ½ lb Ricotta cheese, crumbled
- ¾ cup black olives, chopped
- 10 sun-dried tomatoes, sliced
- 1 tbsp dried oregano
- Black pepper to taste

Directions:

1. Bring to a boil salted water in a pot over high heat. Add the rigatoni and cook according to package directions; drain. Heat the olive oil in a large saucepan over medium heat. Add the rigatoni, ricotta, olives, and sun-dried tomatoes. Toss mixture to combine and cook 2–3 minutes or until cheese just starts to melt. Season with oregano and pepper.

Nutrition Info:
- Per Serving: Calories: 383;Fat: 28g;Protein: 15g;-Carbs: 21g.

Kale Chicken With Pappardelle

Servings:4 | Cooking Time:30 Min + Chilling Time

Ingredients:

- 1 cup grated Parmigiano-Reggiano cheese
- 4 chicken thighs, cut into 1-inch pieces
- 3 tbsp olive oil
- 16 oz pappardelle pasta
- Salt and black pepper to taste
- 1 yellow onion, chopped
- 4 garlic cloves, minced
- 12 cherry tomatoes, halved
- ½ cup chicken broth
- 2 cups baby kale, chopped
- 2 tbsp pine nuts for topping

Directions:

1. In a pot of boiling water, cook the pappardelle pasta for 8-10 minutes until al dente. Drain and set aside.
2. Heat the olive oil in a medium pot. Season the chicken with salt and pepper and sear in the oil until golden brown on the outside. Transfer to a plate and set aside. Add the onion and garlic to the oil and cook until softened and fragrant, 3 minutes. Mix in tomatoes and chicken broth and cook over low heat until the tomatoes soften and the liquid reduces by half. Season with salt and pepper. Return the chicken to the pot and stir in kale. Allow wilting for 2 minutes. Spoon the pappardelle onto serving plates, top with kale sauce and Parmigianino-Reggiano cheese. Garnish with pine nuts.

Nutrition Info:

- Per Serving: Calories: 740;Fat: 53g;Protein: 50g;-Carbs: 15g.

Caprese Pasta With Roasted Asparagus

Servings:6 | Cooking Time: 25 Minutes

Ingredients:

- 8 ounces uncooked small pasta, like orecchiette (little ears) or farfalle (bow ties)
- 1½ pounds fresh asparagus, ends trimmed and stalks chopped into 1-inch pieces
- 1½ cups grape tomatoes, halved
- 2 tablespoons extra-virgin olive oil
- ¼ teaspoon kosher salt
- ¼ teaspoon freshly ground black pepper
- 2 cups fresh Mozzarella, drained and cut into bite-size pieces
- ⅓ cup torn fresh basil leaves
- 2 tablespoons balsamic vinegar

Directions:

1. Preheat the oven to 400ºF.
2. In a large stockpot of salted water, cook the pasta for about 8 to 10 minutes. Drain and reserve about ¼ cup of the cooking liquid.
3. Meanwhile, in a large bowl, toss together the asparagus, tomatoes, oil, salt and pepper. Spread the mixture onto a large, rimmed baking sheet and bake in the oven for 15 minutes, stirring twice during cooking.
4. Remove the vegetables from the oven and add the cooked pasta to the baking sheet. Mix with a few tablespoons of cooking liquid to help the sauce become smoother and the saucy vegetables stick to the pasta.
5. Gently mix in the Mozzarella and basil. Drizzle with the balsamic vinegar. Serve from the baking sheet or pour the pasta into a large bowl.

Nutrition Info:

- Per Serving: Calories: 147;Fat: 3.0g;Protein: 16.0g;-Carbs: 17.0g.

Traditional Beef Lasagna

Servings:4 | Cooking Time:70 Minutes

Ingredients:
- 2 tbsp olive oil
- 1 lb lasagne sheets
- 1 lb ground beef
- 1 white onion, chopped
- 1 tsp Italian seasoning
- Salt and black pepper to taste
- 1 cup marinara sauce
- ½ cup grated Parmesan cheese

Directions:

1. Preheat oven to 350° F. Warm olive oil in a skillet and add the beef and onion. Cook until the beef is brown, 7-8 minutes. Season with Italian seasoning, salt, and pepper. Cook for 1 minute and mix in the marinara sauce. Simmer for 3 minutes.
2. Spread a layer of the beef mixture in a lightly greased baking sheet and make a first single layer on the beef mixture. Top with a single layer of lasagna sheets. Repeat the layering two more times using the remaining ingredients in the same quantities. Sprinkle with Parmesan cheese. Bake in the oven until the cheese melts and is bubbly with the sauce, 20 minutes. Remove the lasagna, allow cooling for 2 minutes and dish onto serving plates. Serve warm.

Nutrition Info:
- Per Serving: Calories: 557;Fat: 29g;Protein: 60g;-Carbs: 4g.

Cherry, Apricot, And Pecan Brown Rice Bowl

Servings:2 | Cooking Time: 1 Hour 1 Minutes

Ingredients:
- 2 tablespoons olive oil
- 2 green onions, sliced
- ½ cup brown rice
- 1 cup low -sodium chicken stock
- 2 tablespoons dried cherries
- 4 dried apricots, chopped
- 2 tablespoons pecans, toasted and chopped
- Sea salt and freshly ground pepper, to taste

Directions:

1. Heat the olive oil in a medium saucepan over medium-high heat until shimmering.
2. Add the green onions and sauté for 1 minutes or until fragrant.
3. Add the rice. Stir to mix well, then pour in the chicken stock.
4. Bring to a boil. Reduce the heat to low. Cover and simmer for 50 minutes or until the brown rice is soft.
5. Add the cherries, apricots, and pecans, and simmer for 10 more minutes or until the fruits are tender.
6. Pour them in a large serving bowl. Fluff with a fork. Sprinkle with sea salt and freshly ground pepper. Serve immediately.

Nutrition Info:
- Per Serving: Calories: 451;Fat: 25.9g;Protein: 8.2g;-Carbs: 50.4g.

Carrot & Caper Chickpeas

Servings:4 | Cooking Time:35 Minutes

Ingredients:
- 3 tbsp olive oil
- 3 tbsp capers, drained
- 1 lemon, juiced and zested
- 1 red onion, chopped
- 14 oz canned chickpeas
- 4 carrots, peeled and cubed
- 1 tbsp parsley, chopped
- Salt and black pepper to taste

Directions:

1. Warm the olive oil in a skillet over medium heat and cook onion, lemon zest, lemon juice, and capers for 5 minutes. Stir in chickpeas, carrots, parsley, salt, and pepper and cook for another 20 minutes. Serve and enjoy!

Nutrition Info:
- Per Serving: Calories: 210;Fat: 5g;Protein: 4g;Carbs: 7g.

Two-bean Cassoulet

Servings:4 | Cooking Time:40 Minutes

Ingredients:
- 2 tbsp olive oil
- 1 cup canned pinto beans
- 1 cup canned can kidney beans
- 2 red bell peppers, chopped
- 1 onion, chopped
- 1 celery stalk, chopped
- 2 garlic cloves, minced
- 1 can diced tomatoes
- 1 tbsp red pepper flakes
- 1 tsp ground cumin
- Salt and black pepper to taste
- ¼ tsp ground coriander

Directions:

1. Warm olive oil in a pot over medium heat and sauté bell peppers, celery, garlic, and onion for 5 minutes until tender. Stir in ground cumin, ground coriander, salt, and pepper for 1 minute. Pour in beans, tomatoes, and red pepper flakes. Bring to a boil, then decrease the heat and simmer for another 20 minutes. Serve immediately.

Nutrition Info:
- Per Serving: Calories: 361;Fat: 8.4g;Protein: 17g;Carbs: 56g.

Parmesan Zucchini Farfalle

Servings:4 | Cooking Time:42 Minutes

Ingredients:
- 3 tbsp olive oil
- 2 garlic cloves, minced
- 4 medium zucchini, diced
- Salt and black pepper to taste
- ½ cup milk
- ¼ tsp ground nutmeg
- 8 oz bow ties
- ½ cup Romano cheese, grated
- 1 tbsp lemon juice

Directions:

1. Heat the oil in a large skillet over medium heat. Stir-fry garlic for 1 minute. Add zucchini, pepper, and salt, stir and cook for 15 minutes, stirring once or twice. In a microwave-safe bowl, warm the milk in the microwave on high for 30 seconds. Stir the milk and nutmeg into the skillet and cook for another 5 minutes, stirring occasionally.

2. Meanwhile, in a large pot, cook the pasta according to the package directions. Drain the pasta in a colander, saving ¼ cup of the pasta liquid. Add the pasta and liquid to the skillet. Mix everything together and remove from the heat. Stir in the grated cheese and lemon juice and serve immediately.

Nutrition Info:
- Per Serving: Calories: 277;Fat: 8g;Protein: 8g;Carbs: 32g.

Freekeh Pilaf With Dates And Pistachios

Servings: 4 | Cooking Time: 10 Minutes

Ingredients:
- 2 tablespoons extra-virgin olive oil, plus extra for drizzling
- 1 shallot, minced
- 1½ teaspoons grated fresh ginger
- ¼ teaspoon ground coriander
- ¼ teaspoon ground cumin
- Salt and pepper, to taste
- 1¾ cups water
- 1½ cups cracked freekeh, rinsed
- 3 ounces pitted dates, chopped
- ¼ cup shelled pistachios, toasted and coarsely chopped
- 1½ tablespoons lemon juice
- ¼ cup chopped fresh mint

Directions:
1. Set the Instant Pot to Sauté mode and heat the olive oil until shimmering.
2. Add the shallot, ginger, coriander, cumin, salt, and pepper to the pot and cook for about 2 minutes, or until the shallot is softened. Stir in the water and freekeh.
3. Secure the lid. Select the Manual mode and set the cooking time for 4 minutes at High Pressure. Once cooking is complete, do a quick pressure release. Carefully open the lid.
4. Add the dates, pistachios and lemon juice and gently fluff the freekeh with a fork to combine. Season to taste with salt and pepper.
5. Transfer to a serving dish and sprinkle with the mint. Serve drizzled with extra olive oil.

Nutrition Info:
- Per Serving: Calories: 280;Fat: 8.0g;Protein: 8.0g;-Carbs: 46.0g.

Lebanese Flavor Broken Thin Noodles

Servings: 6 | Cooking Time: 25 Minutes

Ingredients:
- 1 tablespoon extra-virgin olive oil
- 1 cup vermicelli, broken into 1- to 1½-inch pieces
- 3 cups shredded cabbage
- 1 cup brown rice
- 3 cups low-sodium vegetable soup
- ½ cup water
- 2 garlic cloves, mashed
- ¼ teaspoon sea salt
- ⅛ teaspoon crushed red pepper flakes
- ½ cup coarsely chopped cilantro
- Fresh lemon slices, for serving

Directions:
1. Heat the olive oil in a saucepan over medium-high heat until shimmering.
2. Add the vermicelli and sauté for 3 minutes or until toasted.
3. Add the cabbage and sauté for 4 minutes or until tender.
4. Pour in the brown rice, vegetable soup, and water. Add the garlic and sprinkle with salt and red pepper flakes.
5. Bring to a boil over high heat. Reduce the heat to medium low. Put the lid on and simmer for another 10 minutes.
6. Turn off the heat, then let sit for 5 minutes without opening the lid.
7. Pour them on a large serving platter and spread with cilantro. Squeeze the lemon slices over and serve warm.

Nutrition Info:
- Per Serving: Calories: 127;Fat: 3.1g;Protein: 4.2g;-Carbs: 22.9g.

Sun-dried Tomato & Basil Risotto

Servings:4 | Cooking Time:35 Minutes

Ingredients:

- 10 oz sundried tomatoes in olive oil, drained and chopped
- 2 tbsp olive oil
- 2 cups chicken stock
- 1 onion, chopped
- 1 cup Arborio rice
- Salt and black pepper to taste
- 1 cup Pecorino cheese, grated
- ¼ cup basil leaves, chopped

Directions:

1. Warm the olive oil in a skillet over medium heat and cook onion and sundried tomatoes for 5 minutes. Stir in rice, chicken stock, salt, pepper, and basil and bring to a boil. Cook for 20 minutes. Mix in Pecorino cheese and serve.

Nutrition Info:

- Per Serving: Calories: 430;Fat: 9g;Protein: 8g;Carbs: 57g.

Roasted Pepper Brown Rice

Servings:6 | Cooking Time:1 Hour 50 Minutes

Ingredients:

- 2 tbsp Pecorino-Romano cheese, grated
- ¾ cup roasted red peppers, chopped
- 4 tsp olive oil
- 2 onions, finely chopped
- Salt and black pepper to taste
- 1 ½ cups vegetable broth
- 1 ½ cups brown rice, rinsed
- 1 lemon, cut into wedges

Directions:

1. Preheat oven to 375° F. Heat oil in a pot over medium heat until sizzling. Stir-fry the onions for 10-12 minutes until soft. Season with salt. Stir in 2 cups of water and broth and bring to a boil. Add in rice, cover, and transfer the pot to the oven. Cook until the rice is tender and liquid absorbed, 50-65 minutes. Remove from the oven. Sprinkle with red peppers and let sit for 5 minutes. Season to taste and stir in Pecorino-Romano cheese. Serve with lemon wedges.

Nutrition Info:

- Per Serving: Calories: 308;Fat: 10g;Protein: 11g;-Carbs: 52g.

Authentic Fettuccine A La Puttanesca

Servings:4 | Cooking Time:20 Minutes

Ingredients:

- 2 tbsp extra-virgin olive oil
- 20 Kalamata olives, chopped
- ¼ cup fresh basil, chopped
- 4 garlic cloves, minced
- 2 anchovy fillets, chopped
- ¼ tsp red pepper flakes
- 3 tbsp capers
- 3 cans diced tomatoes
- 8 oz fettuccine pasta
- 2 tbsp Parmesan cheese, grated
- Salt and black pepper to taste

Directions:

1. Cook the fettuccine pasta according to pack instructions, drain and let it to cool. Warm olive oil in a skillet over medium heat and cook garlic and red flakes for 2 minutes. Add in capers, anchovies, olives, salt, and pepper and cook for another 2-3 minutes until the anchovies melt into the oil. Blend tomatoes in a food processor. Pour into the skillet and stir-fry for 5 minutes. Mix in basil and pasta. Serve garnished with Parmesan cheese.

Nutrition Info:

- Per Serving: Calories: 443;Fat: 14g;Protein: 18g;-Carbs: 65g.

Kale & Feta Couscous

Servings: 4 | Cooking Time: 20 Minutes

Ingredients:
- 2 tbsp olive oil
- 1 cup couscous
- 1 cup kale, chopped
- 1 tbsp parsley, chopped
- 3 spring onions, chopped
- 1 cucumber, chopped
- 1 tsp allspice
- ½ lemon, juiced and zested
- 4 oz feta cheese, crumbled

Directions:

1. In a bowl, place couscous and cover with hot water. Let sit for 10 minutes and fluff. Warm the olive oil in a skillet over medium heat and sauté onions and allspice for 3 minutes. Stir in the remaining ingredients and cook for 5-6 minutes.

Nutrition Info:
- Per Serving: Calories: 210;Fat: 7g;Protein: 5g;Carbs: 16g.

Roasted Ratatouille Pasta

Servings: 2 | Cooking Time: 30 Minutes

Ingredients:
- 1 small eggplant
- 1 small zucchini
- 1 portobello mushroom
- 1 Roma tomato, halved
- ½ medium sweet red pepper, seeded
- ½ teaspoon salt, plus additional for the pasta water
- 1 teaspoon Italian herb seasoning
- 1 tablespoon olive oil
- 2 cups farfalle pasta
- 2 tablespoons minced sun-dried tomatoes in olive oil with herbs
- 2 tablespoons prepared pesto

Directions:

1. Slice the ends off the eggplant and zucchini. Cut them lengthwise into ½-inch slices.
2. Place the eggplant, zucchini, mushroom, tomato, and red pepper in a large bowl and sprinkle with ½ teaspoon of salt. Using your hands, toss the vegetables well so that they're covered evenly with the salt. Let them rest for about 10 minutes.
3. While the vegetables are resting, preheat the oven to 400°F. Line a baking sheet with parchment paper.
4. When the oven is hot, drain off any liquid from the vegetables and pat them dry with a paper towel. Add the Italian herb seasoning and olive oil to the vegetables and toss well to coat both sides.
5. Lay the vegetables out in a single layer on the baking sheet. Roast them for 15 to 20 minutes, flipping them over after about 10 minutes or once they start to brown on the underside. When the vegetables are charred in spots, remove them from the oven.
6. While the vegetables are roasting, fill a large saucepan with water. Add salt and cook the pasta until al dente, about 8 to 10 minutes. Drain the pasta, reserving ½ cup of the pasta water.
7. When cool enough to handle, cut the vegetables into large chunks and add them to the hot pasta.
8. Stir in the sun-dried tomatoes and pesto and toss everything well. Serve immediately.

Nutrition Info:
- Per Serving: Calories: 613;Fat: 16.0g;Protein: 23.1g;Carbs: 108.5g.

Fruits, Desserts And Snacks Recipes

Fruits, Desserts And Snacks Recipes

Spicy Hummus

Servings:6 | Cooking Time:10 Minutes

Ingredients:
- 2 tbsp olive oil
- ½ tsp hot paprika
- 1 tsp hot pepper sauce
- 1 tsp ground cumin
- 3 garlic cloves, minced
- 1 can chickpeas
- 2 tbsp tahini
- 2 tbsp chopped fresh parsley
- 1 lemon, juiced and zested
- Salt to taste

Directions:

1. In a food processor, blend chickpeas, tahini, oil, garlic, lemon juice, lemon zest, salt, cumin, and hot pepper sauce for a minute until smooth. Decorate with parsley and paprika.

Nutrition Info:
- Per Serving: Calories: 236;Fat: 8.6g;Protein: 10g;-Carbs: 31g.

Pepperoni Fat Head Pizza

Servings:4 | Cooking Time:35 Minutes

Ingredients:
- 2 tbsp olive oil
- 2 cups flour
- 1 cup lukewarm water
- 1 pinch of sugar
- 1 tsp active dry yeast
- ¾ tsp salt
- 1 tsp dried oregano
- 2 cups mozzarella cheese
- 1 cup sliced pepperoni

Directions:

1. Sift the flour and salt in a bowl and stir in yeast. Mix lukewarm water, olive oil, and sugar in another bowl. Add the wet mixture to the dry mixture and whisk until you obtain a soft dough. Place the dough on a lightly floured work surface and knead it thoroughly for 4-5 minutes until elastic. Transfer the dough to a greased bowl. Cover with cling film and leave to rise for 50-60 minutes in a warm place until doubled in size. Roll out the dough to a thickness of around 12 inches.

2. Preheat oven to 400 °F. Line a round pizza pan with parchment paper. Spread the dough on the pizza pan and top with the mozzarella cheese, oregano, and pepperoni slices. Bake in the oven for 15 minutes or until the cheese melts. Remove the pizza from the oven and let cool slightly. Slice and serve.

Nutrition Info:
- Per Serving: Calories: 229;Fat: 7g;Protein: 36g;-Carbs: 0.4g.

Portuguese Orange Mug Cake

Servings:2 | Cooking Time:12 Minutes

Ingredients:
- 2 tbsp butter, melted
- 6 tbsp flour
- 2 tbsp sugar
- ½ tsp baking powder
- ¼ tsp salt
- 1 tsp orange zest
- 1 egg
- 2 tbsp orange juice
- 2 tbsp milk
- ½ tsp orange extract
- ½ tsp vanilla extract
- Orange slices for garnish

Directions:

1. In a bowl, beat the egg, butter, orange juice, milk, orange extract, and vanilla extract. In another bowl, combine the flour, sugar, baking powder, salt, and orange zest. Pour the dry ingredients into the wet ingredients and stir to combine. Spoon the mixture into 2 mugs and microwave one at a time for 1-2 minutes. Garnish with orange slices.

Nutrition Info:
- Per Serving: Calories: 302;Fat: 17g;Protein: 6g;Carbs: 33g.

Stuffed Cherry Tomatoes

Servings:4 | Cooking Time:10 Minutes

Ingredients:
- 2 tbsp olive oil
- 16 cherry tomatoes
- 1 tbsp lemon zest
- ½ cup feta cheese, crumbled
- 2 tbsp olive tapenade
- ¼ cup parsley, torn

Directions:

1. Using a sharp knife, slice off the tops of the tomatoes and hollow out the insides. Combine olive oil, lemon zest, feta cheese, olive tapenade, and parsley in a bowl. Fill the cherry tomatoes with the feta mixture and arrange them on a plate.

Nutrition Info:
- Per Serving: Calories: 140;Fat: 9g;Protein: 6g;Carbs: 6g.

Baked Balsamic Beet Rounds

Servings:6 | Cooking Time:45 Minutes

Ingredients:
- 4 tbsp olive oil
- 4 beets, peeled, cut into wedges
- Salt and black pepper to taste
- 3 tsp fresh thyme
- ⅓ cup balsamic vinegar
- 1 tbsp fresh dill, chopped

Directions:

1. Preheat oven to 400 °F. Place the beets into a large bowl. Add 2 tbsp of olive oil, salt, and thyme and toss to combine. Spread the beets onto a baking sheet. Bake for 35-40 minutes, turning once or twice until the beets are tender. Remove and let them cool for 10 minutes. In a small bowl, whisk together the remaining olive oil, vinegar, dill, and black pepper. Transfer the beets into a serving bowl, spoon the vinegar mixture over the beets, and serve.

Nutrition Info:
- Per Serving: Calories: 111;Fat: 7g;Protein: 2g;Carbs: 11g.

Chili Grilled Eggplant Rounds

Servings:4 | Cooking Time:25 Minutes

Ingredients:
- 1 cup roasted peppers, chopped
- 4 tbsp olive oil
- 2 eggplants, cut into rounds
- 12 Kalamata olives, chopped
- 1 tsp red chili flakes, crushed
- Salt and black pepper to taste
- 2 tbsp basil, chopped
- 2 tbsp Parmesan cheese, grated

Directions:

1. Combine roasted peppers, half of the olive oil, olives, red chili flakes, salt, and pepper in a bowl. Rub each eggplant slice with remaining olive oil and salt grill them on the preheated grill for 14 minutes on both sides. Remove to a platter. Distribute the pepper mixture across the eggplant rounds and top with basil and Parmesan cheese to serve.

Nutrition Info:
- Per Serving: Calories: 220;Fat: 11g;Protein: 6g;Carbs: 16g.

Crunchy Almond Cookies

Servings: 4 | Cooking Time: 5 To 7 Minutes

Ingredients:
- ½ cup sugar
- 8 tablespoons almond butter
- 1 large egg
- 1½ cups all-purpose flour
- 1 cup ground almonds

Directions:

1. Preheat the oven to 375ºF. Line a baking sheet with parchment paper.
2. Using a mixer, whisk together the sugar and butter. Add the egg and mix until combined. Alternately add the flour and ground almonds, ½ cup at a time, while the mixer is on slow.
3. Drop 1 tablespoon of the dough on the prepared baking sheet, keeping the cookies at least 2 inches apart.
4. Put the baking sheet in the oven and bake for about 5 to 7 minutes, or until the cookies start to turn brown around the edges.
5. Let cool for 5 minutes before serving.

Nutrition Info:
- Per Serving: Calories: 604;Fat: 36.0g;Protein: 11.0g;Carbs: 63.0g.

Fancy Baileys Ice Coffee

Servings: 4 | Cooking Time: 5 Min + Chilling Time

Ingredients:
- 1 cup espresso
- 2 cups milk
- 4 tbsp Baileys
- ½ tsp ground cinnamon
- ½ tsp vanilla extract
- Ice cubes

Directions:

1. Fill four glasses with ice cubes. Mix milk, cinnamon, and vanilla in a food processor until nice and frothy. Pour into the glasses. Combine the Baileys with the espresso and mix well. Pour ¼ of the espresso mixture over the milk and serve.

Nutrition Info:
- Per Serving: Calories: 100;Fat: 5g;Protein: 4g;Carbs: 8g.

Mascarpone Baked Pears

Servings: 2 | Cooking Time: 20 Minutes

Ingredients:
- 2 ripe pears, peeled
- 1 tablespoon plus 2 teaspoons honey, divided
- 1 teaspoon vanilla, divided
- ¼ teaspoon ground coriander
- ¼ teaspoon ginger
- ¼ cup minced walnuts
- ¼ cup mascarpone cheese
- Pinch salt
- Cooking spray

Directions:

1. Preheat the oven to 350ºF. Spray a small baking dish with cooking spray.
2. Slice the pears in half lengthwise. Using a spoon, scoop out the core from each piece. Put the pears, cut side up, in the baking dish.
3. Whisk together 1 tablespoon of honey, ½ teaspoon of vanilla, ginger, and coriander in a small bowl. Pour this mixture evenly over the pear halves.
4. Scatter the walnuts over the pear halves.
5. Bake in the preheated oven for 20 minutes, or until the pears are golden and you're able to pierce them easily with a knife.
6. Meanwhile, combine the mascarpone cheese with the remaining 2 teaspoons of honey, ½ teaspoon of vanilla, and a pinch of salt. Stir to combine well.
7. Divide the mascarpone among the warm pear halves and serve.

Nutrition Info:
- Per Serving: Calories: 308;Fat: 16.0g;Protein: 4.1g;Carbs: 42.7g.

Salt & Pepper Toasted Walnuts

Servings: 6 | Cooking Time: 20 Minutes

Ingredients:

- 2 tbsp olive oil
- 4 cups walnut halves
- Sea salt flakes to taste
- Black pepper to taste

Directions:

1. Preheat the oven to 250 °F. In a bowl, toss the walnuts with olive oil, salt, and pepper to coat. Spread out the walnuts on a parchment-lined baking sheet. Toast for 10-15 minutes. Remove from the oven and allow to cool completely. Serve.

Nutrition Info:

- Per Serving: Calories: 193; Fat: 2g; Protein: 8g; Carbs: 23g.

The Best Anchovy Tapenade

Servings: 4 | Cooking Time: 10 Minutes

Ingredients:

- 1 cup roasted red peppers, chopped
- 3 tbsp olive oil
- 2 anchovy fillets, chopped
- 2 tbsp parsley, chopped
- 14 oz canned artichokes
- ¼ cup capers, drained
- 1 tbsp lemon juice
- 2 garlic cloves, minced

Directions:

1. In a food processor, blend roasted peppers, anchovies, parsley, artichokes, oil, capers, lemon juice, and garlic until a paste is formed. Serve at room temperature

Nutrition Info:

- Per Serving: Calories: 210; Fat: 6g; Protein: 5g; Carbs: 13g.

Spicy Chorizo Pizza

Servings: 4 | Cooking Time: 45 Minutes

Ingredients:

- For the crust
- 2 tbsp olive oil
- 2 cups flour
- 1 cup lukewarm water
- 1 pinch of sugar
- 1 tsp active dry yeast
- ¾ tsp salt
- For the topping
- 1 cup sliced smoked mozzarella cheese
- 1 tbsp olive oil
- 1 cups sliced chorizo
- ¼ cup marinara sauce
- 1 jalapeño pepper, sliced
- ¼ red onion, thinly sliced

Directions:

1. Sift the flour and salt in a bowl and stir in yeast. Mix lukewarm water, olive oil, and sugar in another bowl. Add the wet mixture to the dry mixture and whisk until you obtain a soft dough. Place the dough on a lightly floured work surface and knead it thoroughly for 4-5 minutes until elastic. Transfer the dough to a greased bowl. Cover with cling film and leave to rise for 50-60 minutes in a warm place until doubled in size. Roll out the dough to a thickness of around 12 inches.

2. Preheat the oven to 400 °F. Line a pizza pan with parchment paper. Heat the olive oil and cook the chorizo until brown, 5 minutes. Spread the marinara sauce on the crust, top with the mozzarella cheese, chorizo, jalapeño pepper, and onion. Bake in the oven until the cheese melts, 15 minutes. Remove from the oven, slice, and serve warm.

Nutrition Info:

- Per Serving: Calories: 391; Fat: 17g; Protein: 11g; Carbs: 51g.

Quick & Easy Red Dip

Servings:4 | Cooking Time:10 Minutes

Ingredients:

- 1 cup roasted red peppers, chopped
- 3 tbsp olive oil
- 1 lb tomatoes, chopped
- Salt and black pepper to taste
- 1 ½ tsp balsamic vinegar
- ½ tsp oregano, chopped
- 2 garlic cloves, minced
- 2 tbsp parsley, chopped

Directions:

1. In a food processor, blend tomatoes, red peppers, salt, pepper, vinegar, oregano, olive oil, garlic, and parsley until smooth. Store this in the fridge for a few days, up to a week.

Nutrition Info:

- Per Serving: Calories: 130;Fat: 5g;Protein: 4g;Carbs: 4g.

Mini Cucumber & Cream Cheese Sandwiches

Servings:4 | Cooking Time:5 Minutes

Ingredients:

- 4 bread slices
- 1 cucumber, sliced
- 2 tbsp cream cheese, soft
- 1 tbsp chives, chopped
- ¼ cup hummus
- Salt and black pepper to taste

Directions:

1. In a bowl, mix hummus, cream cheese, chives, salt, and pepper until well combined. Spread the mixture onto bread slices. Top with cucumber and cut each sandwich into three pieces. Serve immediately.

Nutrition Info:

- Per Serving: Calories: 190;Fat: 13g;Protein: 9g;-Carbs: 5g.

Grilled Peaches With Whipped Ricotta

Servings:4 | Cooking Time: 14 To 22 Minutes

Ingredients:

- 4 peaches, halved and pitted
- 2 teaspoons extra-virgin olive oil
- ¾ cup whole-milk Ricotta cheese
- 1 tablespoon honey
- ¼ teaspoon freshly grated nutmeg
- 4 sprigs mint
- Cooking spray

Directions:

1. Spritz a grill pan with cooking spray. Heat the grill pan to medium heat.
2. Place a large, empty bowl in the refrigerator to chill.
3. Brush the peaches all over with the oil. Place half of the peaches, cut-side down, on the grill pan and cook for 3 to 5 minutes, or until grill marks appear.
4. Using tongs, turn the peaches over. Cover the grill pan with aluminum foil and cook for 4 to 6 minutes, or until the peaches are easily pierced with a sharp knife. Set aside to cool. Repeat with the remaining peaches.
5. Remove the bowl from the refrigerator and add the Ricotta. Using an electric beater, beat the Ricotta on high for 2 minutes. Add the honey and nutmeg and beat for 1 more minute.
6. Divide the cooled peaches among 4 serving bowls. Top with the Ricotta mixture and a sprig of mint and serve.

Nutrition Info:

- Per Serving: Calories: 176;Fat: 8.0g;Protein: 8.0g;-Carbs: 20.0g.

Simple Apple Compote

Servings: 4 | Cooking Time: 10 Minutes

Ingredients:

- 6 apples, peeled, cored, and chopped
- ¼ cup raw honey
- 1 teaspoon ground cinnamon
- ¼ cup apple juice
- Sea salt, to taste

Directions:

1. Put all the ingredients in a stockpot. Stir to mix well, then cook over medium-high heat for 10 minutes or until the apples are glazed by honey and lightly saucy. Stir constantly.
2. Serve immediately.

Nutrition Info:

- Per Serving: Calories: 246;Fat: 0.9g;Protein: 1.2g;Carbs: 66.3g.

Energy Granola Bites

Servings: 5 | Cooking Time: 10 Minutes

Ingredients:

- ¾ cup diced dried figs
- ½ cup chopped walnuts
- ¼ cup old-fashioned oats
- 2 tbsp ground flaxseed
- 2 tbsp peanut butter
- 2 tbsp honey

Directions:

1. In a medium bowl, mix together the figs, walnuts, oats, flaxseed, and peanut butter. Drizzle with the honey, and mix everything with a wooden spoon. Freeze the dough for 5 minutes. Divide the dough evenly into four sections in the bowl. Dampen your hands with water—but don't get them too wet, or the dough will stick to them. With hands, roll three bites out of each of the four sections of dough, making 10 energy bites. Store in the fridge for up to a week.

Nutrition Info:

- Per Serving: Calories: 158;Fat: 8g;Protein: 3g;Carbs: 23g.

Ultimate Seed Crackers

Servings: 6 | Cooking Time: 20 Minutes

Ingredients:

- 1 cup almond flour
- 1 tbsp sesame seeds
- 1 tbsp sunflower seeds
- 1 tbsp flaxseed
- 1 tbsp chia seeds
- ¼ tsp baking soda
- Salt and black pepper to taste
- 1 egg, beaten

Directions:

1. Preheat oven to 350 °F. In a bowl, mix the almond flour, sesame seeds, flaxseed, chia seeds, sunflower seeds, baking soda, salt, and pepper and stir well. Add the egg and stir well to combine and form the dough into a ball. Place one layer of parchment paper on your counter-top and place the dough on top. Cover with a second layer of parchment and, using a rolling pin, roll the dough to ¼-inch thickness, aiming for a rectangular shape. Cut the dough into crackers and bake on parchment until crispy and slightly golden, 10-15 minutes, depending on thickness. Alternatively, you can bake the large rolled dough before cutting and break into free-form crackers once baked and crispy. Store in an airtight container for up to 1 week.

Nutrition Info:

- Per Serving: Calories: 119;Fat: 9g;Protein: 4g;Carbs: 5g.

Berry And Rhubarb Cobbler

Servings: 8 | Cooking Time: 35 Minutes

Ingredients:
- Cobbler:
- 1 cup fresh raspberries
- 2 cups fresh blueberries
- 1 cup sliced (½-inch) rhubarb pieces
- 1 tablespoon arrowroot powder
- ¼ cup unsweetened apple juice
- 2 tablespoons melted coconut oil
- ¼ cup raw honey
- Topping:
- 1 cup almond flour
- 1 tablespoon arrowroot powder
- ½ cup shredded coconut
- ¼ cup raw honey
- ½ cup coconut oil

Directions:
1. Make the Cobbler
2. Preheat the oven to 350°F. Grease a baking dish with melted coconut oil.
3. Combine the ingredients for the cobbler in a large bowl. Stir to mix well.
4. Spread the mixture in the single layer on the baking dish. Set aside.
5. Make the Topping
6. Combine the almond flour, arrowroot powder, and coconut in a bowl. Stir to mix well.
7. Fold in the honey and coconut oil. Stir with a fork until the mixture crumbled.
8. Spread the topping over the cobbler, then bake in the preheated oven for 35 minutes or until frothy and golden brown.
9. Serve immediately.

Nutrition Info:
- Per Serving: Calories: 305;Fat: 22.1g;Protein: 3.2g;-Carbs: 29.8g.

Parsley Lamb Arancini

Servings: 4 | Cooking Time: 25 Minutes

Ingredients:
- 3 tbsp olive oil
- 1 lb ground lamb
- ½ tsp cumin, ground
- 1 garlic clove, minced
- Salt and black pepper to taste
- 1 cup rice
- 2 cups vegetable broth
- ¼ cup parsley, chopped
- ¼ cup shallots, chopped
- ½ tsp allspice
- 2 eggs, lightly beaten
- 1 cup breadcrumbs

Directions:
1. Cook the rice in the vegetable broth for about 15 minutes. Remove from the heat and leave to cool uncovered. In a large bowl, mix the cooled rice, ground lamb, cumin, garlic, salt, pepper, parsley, shallots, and allspice until combined. Form medium balls out of the mixture. Dip the arancini in the beaten eggs and toss in the breadcrumbs. Warm the olive oil in a skillet over medium heat and fry meatballs for 14 minutes on all sides until golden brown. Remove to paper towels to absorb excess oil. Serve warm.

Nutrition Info:
- Per Serving: Calories: 310;Fat: 10g;Protein: 7g;-Carbs: 23g.

Chickpea & Spinach Salad With Almonds

Servings:4 | Cooking Time:5 Minutes

Ingredients:
- 2 tbsp olive oil
- 3 spring onions, chopped
- 1 cup baby spinach
- 15 oz canned chickpeas
- Salt and black pepper to taste
- 2 tbsp lemon juice
- 1 tbsp cilantro, chopped
- 2 tbsp almonds flakes, toasted

Directions:
1. Toss chickpeas, spring onions, spinach, salt, pepper, olive oil, lemon juice, and cilantro in a salad bowl. Top with almond flakes. Serve and enjoy!

Nutrition Info:
- Per Serving: Calories: 230;Fat: 6g;Protein: 16g;-Carbs: 10g.

Easy Blueberry And Oat Crisp

Servings:4 | Cooking Time: 20 Minutes

Ingredients:
- 2 tablespoons coconut oil, melted, plus additional for greasing
- 4 cups fresh blueberries
- Juice of ½ lemon
- 2 teaspoons lemon zest
- ¼ cup maple syrup
- 1 cup gluten-free rolled oats
- ½ cup chopped pecans
- ½ teaspoon ground cinnamon
- Sea salt, to taste

Directions:
1. Preheat the oven to 350ºF. Grease a baking sheet with coconut oil.
2. Combine the blueberries, lemon juice and zest, and maple syrup in a bowl. Stir to mix well, then spread the mixture on the baking sheet.
3. Combine the remaining ingredients in a small bowl. Stir to mix well. Pour the mixture over the blueberries mixture.
4. Bake in the preheated oven for 20 minutes or until the oats are golden brown.
5. Serve immediately with spoons.

Nutrition Info:
- Per Serving: Calories: 496;Fat: 32.9g;Protein: 5.1g;-Carbs: 50.8g.

Rice Pudding With Roasted Orange

Servings:6 | Cooking Time: 19 To 20 Minutes

Ingredients:
- 2 medium oranges
- 2 teaspoons extra-virgin olive oil
- ⅛ teaspoon kosher salt
- 2 large eggs
- 2 cups unsweetened almond milk
- 1 cup orange juice
- 1 cup uncooked instant brown rice
- ¼ cup honey
- ½ teaspoon ground cinnamon
- 1 teaspoon vanilla extract
- Cooking spray

Directions:
1. Preheat the oven to 450ºF. Spritz a large, rimmed baking sheet with cooking spray. Set aside.
2. Slice the unpeeled oranges into ¼-inch rounds. Brush with the oil and sprinkle with salt. Place the slices on the baking sheet and roast for 4 minutes. Flip the slices and roast for 4 more minutes, or until they begin to brown. Remove from the oven and set aside.
3. Crack the eggs into a medium bowl. In a medium saucepan, whisk together the milk, orange juice, rice, honey and cinnamon. Bring to a boil over medium-high heat, stirring constantly. Reduce the heat to medium-low and simmer for 10 minutes, stirring occasionally.
4. Using a measuring cup, scoop out ½ cup of the hot rice mixture and whisk it into the eggs. While constantly stirring the mixture in the pan, slowly pour the egg mixture back into the saucepan. Cook on low heat for 1 to 2 minutes, or until thickened, stirring constantly. Remove from the heat and stir in the vanilla.
5. Let the pudding stand for a few minutes for the rice to soften. The rice will be cooked but slightly chewy. For softer rice, let stand for another half hour.
6. Top with the roasted oranges. Serve warm or at room temperature.

Nutrition Info:
- Per Serving: Calories: 204;Fat: 6.0g;Protein: 5.0g;-Carbs: 34.0g.

Orange Pannacotta With Blackberries

Servings: 2 | Cooking Time: 15 Min + Chilling Time

Ingredients:

- ¾ cup half-and-half
- 1 tsp powdered gelatin
- ½ cup heavy cream
- 3 tbsp sugar
- 1 tsp orange zest
- 1 tbsp orange juice
- 1 tsp orange extract
- ½ cup fresh blackberries
- 2 mint leaves

Directions:

1. Put ¼ cup of half-and-half in a bowl. Mix in gelatin powder and set it aside for 10 minutes to hydrate. In a saucepan over medium heat, combine the remaining half-and-half, heavy cream, sugar, orange zest, orange juice, and orange extract. Warm the mixture for 4 minutes. Don't let it come to a full boil. Remove from the heat. Let cool slightly.

2. Add the gelatin into the cream mixture and whisk until the gelatin melts. Pour the mixture into 2 dessert glasses and refrigerate for at least 2 hours. Serve with fresh berries and garnish with mint leaves.

Nutrition Info:

- Per Serving: Calories: 422; Fat: 33g; Protein: 6g;-Carbs: 28g.

Skillet Pesto Pizza

Servings: 2 | Cooking Time: 10 Minutes

Ingredients:

- 1 tbsp butter
- 2 pieces of focaccia bread
- 2 tbsp pesto
- 1 medium tomato, sliced
- 2 large eggs

Directions:

1. Place a large skillet over medium heat. Place the focaccia in the skillet and let it warm for about 4 minutes on both sides until softened and just starting to turn golden. Remove to a platter. Spread 1 tablespoon of the pesto on one side of each slice. Cover with tomato slices. Melt the butter in the skillet over medium heat. Crack in the eggs, keeping them separated, and cook until the whites are no longer translucent and the yolk is cooked to desired doneness. Spoon one egg onto each pizza. Serve and enjoy!

Nutrition Info:

- Per Serving: Calories: 427; Fat: 17g; Protein: 17g;-Carbs: 10g.

Fruit Skewers With Vanilla Labneh

Servings: 4 | Cooking Time: 15 Min + Straining Time

Ingredients:

- 2 cups plain yogurt
- 2 tbsp honey
- 1 tsp vanilla extract
- A pinch of salt
- 2 mangoes, cut into chunks

Directions:

1. Place a fine sieve lined with cheesecloth over a bowl and spoon the yogurt into the sieve. Allow the liquid to drain off for 12-24 hours hours. Transfer the strained yogurt to a bowl and mix in the honey, vanilla, and salt. Set it aside.

2. Heat your grill to medium-high. Thread the fruit onto skewers and grill for 2 minutes on each side until the fruit is softened and has grill marks on each side. Serve with labneh.

Nutrition Info:

- Per Serving: Calories: 292; Fat: 6g; Protein: 5g; Carbs: 60g.

Charred Maple Pineapple

Servings: 4 | Cooking Time: 10 Minutes

Ingredients:
- 1 pineapple, peeled and cut into wedges
- 1 tbsp maple syrup
- ½ tsp ground cinnamon

Directions:

1. Preheat a grill pan over high heat. Place the fruit in a bowl and drizzle with maple syrup; sprinkle with ground cinnamon. Grill for about 7-8 minutes, turning occasionally until the fruit chars slightly. Serve.

Nutrition Info:
- Per Serving: Calories: 130;Fat: 0g;Protein: 1g;Carbs: 32g.

Lebanese Spicy Baba Ganoush

Servings: 4 | Cooking Time: 50 Minutes

Ingredients:
- 2 tbsp olive oil
- 2 eggplants, poked with a fork
- 2 tbsp tahini paste
- 1 tsp cayenne pepper
- 2 tbsp lemon juice
- 2 garlic cloves, minced
- Salt and black pepper to taste
- 1 tbsp parsley, chopped

Directions:

1. Preheat oven to 380 °F. Arrange eggplants on a roasting pan and bake for 40 minutes. Set aside to cool. Peel the cooled eggplants and place them in a blender along with the tahini paste, lemon juice, garlic, cayenne pepper, salt, and pepper. Puree the ingredients while gradually adding olive oil until a smooth and homogeneous consistency. Top with parsley.

Nutrition Info:
- Per Serving: Calories: 130;Fat: 5g;Protein: 5g;Carbs: 2g.

30 Day Meal Plan

	Breakfast	Lunch	Dinner
Day 1	Feta & Olive Breakfast	Spicy Cod Fillets	Sun-dried Tomato & Spinach Pasta Salad
Day 2	Classic Shakshuka	Easy Pork Souvlaki	Zesty Asparagus Salad
Day 3	Yummy Lentil Stuffed Pitas	Pork Butt With Leeks	Cucumber & Tomato Salad With Anchovies
Day 4	Baked Eggs In Avocado	Baked Oysters With Vegetables	Moroccan Spinach & Lentil Soup
Day 5	Veg Mix And Blackeye Pea Burritos	Beef, Tomato, And Lentils Stew	Simple Honey-glazed Baby Carrots
Day 6	Red Pepper Coques With Pine Nuts	Chicken Sausages With Pepper Sauce	Parmesan Stuffed Zucchini Boats
Day 7	Mushroom And Caramelized Onion Musakhan	Shrimp & Salmon In Tomato Sauce	Sweet Mustard Cabbage Hash
Day 8	Morning Pizza Frittata	Eggplant & Chicken Skillet	Moroccan Tagine With Vegetables
Day 9	Hot Zucchini & Egg Nests	Roasted Herby Chicken	Rainbow Vegetable Kebabs
Day 10	Tomato Eggs With Fried Potatoes	Baked Anchovies With Chili-garlic Topping	Minty Broccoli & Walnuts
Day 11	Basil Cheese Omelet	Eggplant & Turkey Moussaka	Spicy Roasted Tomatoes
Day 12	Citrus French Toasts	Greek-style Chicken & Vegetable Stir-fry	Zucchini Crisp
Day 13	Lemon Cardamom Buckwheat Pancakes	Fennel & Bell Pepper Salmon	Mini Crustless Spinach Quiches
Day 14	Strawberry Basil Mascarpone Toast	Beef & Pumpkin Stew	Veggie-stuffed Portabello Mushrooms
Day 15	Berry-yogurt Smoothie	Pork Loaf With Colby Cheese	Cauliflower Cakes With Goat Cheese

	Breakfast	Lunch	Dinner
Day 16	Chocolate-strawberry Smoothie	Salmon Stuffed Peppers	Baked Honey Acorn Squash
Day 17	Cheesy Broccoli And Mushroom Egg Casserole	Chicken Tagine With Vegetables	Grilled Eggplant "steaks" With Sauce
Day 18	Couscous & Cucumber Bowl	Beef Filet Mignon In Mushroom Sauce	Parsley & Olive Zucchini Bake
Day 19	Mango-yogurt Smoothie	Salmon And Mushroom Hash With Pesto	Tradicional Matchuba Green Beans
Day 20	Cherry Tomato & Mushroom Frittata	Saucy Turkey With Ricotta Cheese	Baked Vegetable Stew
Day 21	Avocado & Peach Power Smoothie	Chicken Thighs Al Orange	Creamy Polenta With Mushrooms
Day 22	Za'atar Pizza	Baked Cod With Lemony Rice	Spicy Kale With Almonds
Day 23	Easy Pizza Pockets	Marsala Chicken Cacciatore Stir-fry	Simple Broccoli With Yogurt Sauce
Day 24	Tomato And Egg Breakfast Pizza	Beef & Bell Pepper Bake	Homemade Vegetarian Moussaka
Day 25	Mediterranean Omelet	Spicy Haddock Stew	Chickpea Lettuce Wraps With Celery
Day 26	Zucchini & Tomato Cheese Tart	Chicken Drumsticks With Peach Glaze	Eggplant Rolls In Tomato Sauce
Day 27	Zucchini Hummus Wraps	Homemade Pizza Burgers	Spinach & Lentil Stew
Day 28	Pesto Salami & Cheese Egg Cupcakes	Shrimp And Pea Paella	Balsamic Grilled Vegetables
Day 29	Tasty Lentil Burgers	Roasted Pork Tenderloin With Apple Sauce	Roasted Artichokes
Day 30	Mustard Sardine Cakes	Tangy Mushroom & Chicken Kabobs	Baked Potato With Veggie Mix

Appendix : Recipes Index

A

Anchovy Spread With Avocado   36
Asparagus & Chicken Skillet   54
Authentic Fettuccine A La Puttanesca   75
Avocado & Peach Power Smoothie   17

B

Baby Spinach & Apple Salad With Walnuts   60
Baked Anchovies With Chili-garlic Topping   34
Baked Balsamic Beet Rounds   79
Baked Cod With Lemony Rice   37
Baked Eggs In Avocado   11
Baked Honey Acorn Squash   26
Baked Oysters With Vegetables   33
Baked Potato With Veggie Mix   21
Baked Vegetable Stew   26
Balsamic Grilled Vegetables   21
Balsamic-honey Glazed Salmon   43
Basil Cheese Omelet   14
Beef & Bell Pepper Bake   46
Beef & Pumpkin Stew   49
Beef Filet Mignon In Mushroom Sauce   48
Beef, Tomato, And Lentils Stew   52
Berry And Rhubarb Cobbler   84
Berry-yogurt Smoothie   15
Better-for-you Cod & Potatoes   39
Bolognese Penne Bake   70
Brussels Sprout And Apple Slaw   58

C

Caprese Pasta With Roasted Asparagus   71
Carrot & Caper Chickpeas   73
Cauliflower Cakes With Goat Cheese   27
Charred Maple Pineapple   87
Cheesy Broccoli And Mushroom Egg Casserole   16
Cherry Tomato & Mushroom Frittata   17
Cherry, Apricot, And Pecan Brown Rice Bowl   72
Chicken Cacciatore   53
Chicken Drumsticks With Peach Glaze   46

Chicken Sausages With Pepper Sauce   51
Chicken Tagine With Vegetables   48
Chicken Thighs Al Orange   47
Chickpea & Spinach Salad With Almonds   85
Chickpea Lettuce Wraps With Celery   23
Chili Grilled Eggplant Rounds   79
Chocolate-strawberry Smoothie   15
Citrus French Toasts   14
Classic Aioli   63
Classic Potato Salad With Green Onions   58
Classic Shakshuka   10
Cod Fettuccine   41
Collard Green & Rice Salad   59
Couscous & Cucumber Bowl   16
Cranberry & Walnut Freekeh Pilaf   68
Creamy Polenta With Mushrooms   25
Crunchy Almond Cookies   80
Cucumber & Tomato Salad With Anchovies   56

D

Deluxe Chicken With Yogurt Sauce   53

E

Easy Blueberry And Oat Crisp   85
Easy Pizza Pockets   17
Easy Pork Souvlaki   52
Easy Tomato Tuna Melts   42
Easy Walnut And Ricotta Spaghetti   66
Eggplant & Chicken Skillet   51
Eggplant & Turkey Moussaka   50
Eggplant Casserole With Pecorino Cheese   63
Eggplant Rolls In Tomato Sauce   22
Energy Granola Bites   83

F

Fancy Baileys Ice Coffee   80
Fennel & Bell Pepper Salmon   36
Feta & Olive Breakfast   10
Florentine Bean & Vegetable Gratin   69
Freekeh Pilaf With Dates And Pistachios   74
Fruit Skewers With Vanilla Labneh   86

G

Greek Chicken, Tomato, And Olive Salad 61
Greek-style Chicken & Vegetable Stir-fry 49
Green Beans With Tahini-lemon Sauce 64
Green Pea & Cavolo Nero Farro Pilaf 70
Grilled Bell Pepper And Anchovy Antipasto 57
Grilled Chicken Breasts With Italian Sauce 53
Grilled Eggplant "steaks" With Sauce 26
Grilled Peaches With Whipped Ricotta 82
Grilled Sardines With Herby Sauce 42

H

Herby Beef Soup 51
Homemade Pizza Burgers 46
Homemade Vegetarian Moussaka 24
Hot Zucchini & Egg Nests 14

I

Italian Spinach & Rice Soup 59

K

Kale & Feta Couscous 76
Kale Chicken With Pappardelle 71

L

Lebanese Flavor Broken Thin Noodles 74
Lebanese Spicy Baba Ganoush 87
Leek & Shrimp Soup 60
Lemon Cardamom Buckwheat Pancakes 15
Lemon-parsley Swordfish 41
Lemony Shrimp With Orzo Salad 35

M

Mango-yogurt Smoothie 16
Marsala Chicken Cacciatore Stir-fry 47
Mascarpone Baked Pears 80
Mascarpone Sweet Potato Mash 60
Mediterranean Omelet 19
Mini Crustless Spinach Quiches 28

Mini Cucumber & Cream Cheese Sandwiches 82
Minty Broccoli & Walnuts 29
Morning Pizza Frittata 12
Moroccan Spinach & Lentil Soup 57
Moroccan Tagine With Vegetables 29
Mushroom And Caramelized Onion Musakhan 13
Mushroom And Soba Noodle Soup 62
Mustard Sardine Cakes 36

O

Orange Pannacotta With Blackberries 86
Orange-honey Glazed Carrots 57

P

Paprika Spinach & Chickpea Bowl 68
Parmesan Beef Rotini With Asparagus 68
Parmesan Roasted Red Potatoes 63
Parmesan Stuffed Zucchini Boats 30
Parmesan Zucchini Farfalle 73
Parsley & Olive Zucchini Bake 25
Parsley Lamb Arancini 84
Parsley Littleneck Clams In Sherry Sauce 33
Parsley Tomato Tilapia 41
Parsley Turkish Chicken Soup 62
Pecorino Zucchini Strips 64
Pepperoni Fat Head Pizza 78
Pesto Salami & Cheese Egg Cupcakes 19
Pine Nut & Raisin Spinach 61
Pork Butt With Leeks 52
Pork Loaf With Colby Cheese 49
Portuguese Orange Mug Cake 79

Q

Quick & Easy Red Dip 82

R

Rainbow Vegetable Kebabs 30
Raspberry & Nut Quinoa 67
Red Pepper Coques With Pine Nuts 12
Rice Pudding With Roasted Orange 85
Rich Chicken And Small Pasta Broth 64

Ricotta & Olive Rigatoni   70
Roasted Artichokes   21
Roasted Cherry Tomato & Fennel   61
Roasted Herby Chicken   50
Roasted Pepper Brown Rice   75
Roasted Pork Tenderloin With Apple Sauce   45
Roasted Ratatouille Pasta   76
Roasted Red Snapper With Citrus Topping   34
Root Vegetable Roast   62

S

Salmon And Mushroom Hash With Pesto   37
Salmon Packets   43
Salmon Stuffed Peppers   36
Salt & Pepper Toasted Walnuts   81
Saucy Turkey With Ricotta Cheese   47
Seafood Stew   40
Shrimp & Salmon In Tomato Sauce   35
Shrimp And Pea Paella   38
Sicilian-style Squid With Zucchini   39
Simple Apple Compote   83
Simple Broccoli With Yogurt Sauce   23
Simple Honey-glazed Baby Carrots   31
Skillet Pesto Pizza   86
Spanish-style Linguine With Tapenade   69
Spicy Chorizo Pizza   81
Spicy Cod Fillets   34
Spicy Haddock Stew   38
Spicy Hummus   78
Spicy Kale With Almonds   24
Spicy Roasted Tomatoes   29
Spinach & Lentil Stew   22
Spinach Farfalle With Ricotta Cheese   67
Strawberry Basil Mascarpone Toast   15
Stuffed Cherry Tomatoes   79
Summer Gazpacho   60
Sun-dried Tomato & Basil Risotto   75
Sun-dried Tomato & Spinach Pasta Salad   56
Sweet Mustard Cabbage Hash   30
Sweet Potatoes Stuffed With Beans   66

T

Tangy Mushroom & Chicken Kabobs   45
Tasty Lentil Burgers   31
Tender Pork Shoulder   54

The Best Anchovy Tapenade   81
Thyme Hake With Potatoes   40
Tomato And Egg Breakfast Pizza   18
Tomato Eggs With Fried Potatoes   13
Tomato Sauce And Basil Pesto Fettuccine   67
Tradicional Matchuba Green Beans   24
Traditional Beef Lasagna   72
Tricolor Summer Salad   58
Turmeric Green Bean & Chicken Bake   54
Two-bean Cassoulet   73
Tzatziki Chicken Loaf   50

U

Ultimate Seed Crackers   83

V

Valencian-style Mussel Rice   69
Veg Mix And Blackeye Pea Burritos   11
Veggie-stuffed Portabello Mushrooms   27

W

Walnut-crusted Salmon   39
Wine-steamed Clams   41

Y

Yummy Lentil Stuffed Pitas   10

Z

Za'atar Pizza   17
Zesty Asparagus Salad   56
Zoodles With Beet Pesto   23
Zoodles With Tomato-mushroom Sauce   59
Zucchini & Tomato Cheese Tart   18
Zucchini Crisp   28
Zucchini Hummus Wraps   19

Made in the USA
Las Vegas, NV
19 March 2023